Contents

Introduction

BY DON GREEN
Executive Director
The Napoleon Hill Foundation

Did you ever wonder why success has been possible for some people and seems to elude others? This was a question that Napoleon Hill had in his early childhood and spent his lifetime pursuing that age old question. Hill sought the answer as to why some are successful and millions are not in a manner that no one had ever done before.

Oliver Napoleon Hill was born in 1883 in the remote mountains of Southwest, Virginia. There appeared to be nothing in his early life that would predict Hill to being a success. Born in a log cabin he once said, "For three generations my people had been born, lived, struggled in ignorance and poverty and died without having been outside the mountains of that section."

Life was very primitive when compared to larger cities in the east. Life expectancies were short with a high mortality rate. Many rural Virginians suffered from chronic health problems often caused by inadequate diet.

With little apparent reason to expect success to any large degree, at the early age of 10 Hill lost his mother who was only 26 years old at her death. One year later Napoleon's father remarried which was a turning point in the young boy's life. Napoleon's stepmother, Martha Ramey Banner, was an educated woman, the widow of a high school principal and the daughter of a doctor. Hill's new mother saw potential in him that nobody else seemed to appreciate. At an early age a gun had been traded for a typewriter and Napoleon's stepmother taught him how to use it. The typewriter was used by Hill to type news stories by the age of fifteen and proved to be invaluable throughout his life.

Schools were in critical shape except for the major towns and cities throughout the state. In the mountainous area elementary schools were open only about four months of the year and attendance was not required.

High schools were rare with only about one hundred in the entire state and most offered only a two or three year curriculum. Twenty years after Hill's birth there were only 10 four-year high school programs in all of Virginia. It would be remarkable that he could ever escape such a background, become such a success and influence millions of people in all parts of the world.

Hill often referred to his early childhood in his articles, books and speeches. His recollection of each of his early childhood memories were mostly negative and it is little wonder that Hill often related to his rags-to-riches throughout most of his career.

Finishing high school in Wise, Virginia–a two year program, Hill began to see himself as an executive. Entering a business college in nearby Tazewell, he took courses to prepare for the job of secretary which would help prepare him for the business world.

Hill chose to apply for a job with one of the most successful men living in the Southwest Virginia Mountains. Hill says he offered to work for the job paying the employer during a trial period.

General Rufus Ayres, one of the richest and most successful individuals was to be Napoleon's new employer.

It is easy to understand why Napoleon Hill with his background of being surrounded by poverty and ignorance would want to work for General Ayres.

After Hill had completed a business college course, he wrote to Ayres:

> "I have just completed a business course and am well qualified to serve as your secretary, a position I am very anxious to have.
>
> "Because I have no previous experience, I know

> that at the beginning working for you will be of more value to me than it will be to you. Because of this I am willing to pay for the privilege of working with you.
>
> "You may charge any sum you consider fair, provided at the end of three months that amount will become my salary. The sum that I am to pay you can be deducted from what you pay me when I start to earn money."

Ayres hired young Napoleon who came early, stayed late, and worked–willing "to go the extra mile" to render more service than compensated for. Going the extra mile would become one of Hill's principles for success.

Ayres had the background that would serve Hill well when he began his study of successful individuals and what led to their success. Ayres as a young man served in the Confederate Army in the Civil War. After the war, Ayres worked in a mercantile store and read law where he became a very successful lawyer serving as Attorney General for the state of Virginia. A successful business man, he helped organize banks, operate coal mines and other business ventures. It was from Ayres that Hill got the idea to attend law school to become an attorney.

Hill convinced his brother, Vivian that once accepted to Georgetown University that Hill could use his passion for writing, and support the both of them through college.

The information Hill gathered would lead to a life of writing and speaking on his findings on personal achievement. Hill's findings produced the basics for the eight volume set of *Law of Success* published in 1928 and *Think and Grow Rich* in 1937, the best selling self-help book of all time.

The book you are about to read will provide you with valuable writings on success before Hill published his first book. Remember it was 1908 when Hill interviewed Andrew Carnegie, but twenty years before he published his first book.

During this twenty year period Hill was writing, speaking, teaching classes on the principles, and publishing his own magazine. Hill published Napoleon Hill's Magazine and Napoleon Hill's Golden Rule Magazine. Articles from these magazines compose the book you are holding and give valuable insight to some of Hill's earliest writings, whether you are a reader of Hill's famous works or this is your first time of reading Hill's writings, you will gain valuable insight that will help you in life.

Hill secured a job with Bob Taylor's Magazine. The year was 1908, an assignment sent Hill to New York to interview Andrew Carnegie at his 64 room mansion. Carnegie had come to the United States as a youth with very little schooling. Through hard work and investments Carnegie became a millionaire at an early age. As the founder of US Steel, Carnegie was 74 years old when Hill interviewed him. Carnegie had given away 350 million dollars from his sale of US Steel by the time of his death in 1919.

Carnegie talked about principles of achievement to Hill. Before the conversation was over, Carnegie challenged him to interview and study the lives of great leaders. Finally he compiled his findings into a set of principles in order that other people could be helped to help themselves and realize their dreams.

Carnegie furnished Hill with the introduction to the leaders of the time such as John D. Rockefeller, Thomas Edison, Henry Ford, George Eastman and others. You will discover why Hill's work is more popular all over the world and has influenced the present self-help movement like no other in history.

ROAD TO SUCCESS

The Classic Guide for Prosperity and Happiness

Putting the Principles of *Think and Grow Rich* into Action in Your Life

THE NAPOLEON HILL FOUNDATION

NAPOLEON HILL

Introduction by Don Green

JAICO PUBLISHING HOUSE

Ahmedabad Bangalore Bhopal Bhubaneswar Chennai
Delhi Hyderabad Kolkata Lucknow Mumbai

Published by Jaico Publishing House
A-2 Jash Chambers, 7-A Sir Phirozshah Mehta Road
Fort, Mumbai - 400 001
jaicopub@jaicobooks.com
www.jaicobooks.com

Published in arrangement with
The Napoleon Hill Foundation
1 College Avenue, Wise
Virginia 24293, USA

ROAD TO SUCCESS
ISBN 978-81-8495-257-5

First Jaico Impression: 2011
11th Jaico Impression: 2019

Printed by
Concept Imprint Pvt. Ltd., Ghaziabad, (U.P.)

Preface

BY THE NAPOLEON HILL FOUNDATION

It was 1908 when the young writer Napoleon Hill interviewed U.S. Steel founder, Andrew Carnegie and accepted his offer to study successful individuals. Carnegie told Hill "a philosophy of success would help others become successful." Hill gladly accepted the twenty-year assignment in order to develop and teach the philosophy of success. Hill remarked in one of his lectures that when Carnegie spoke of philosophy of success that he went to a library to find out what the word PHILOSOPHY meant.

While living in Washington D.C. in 1910 he received the assignment to travel to Detroit to interview Henry Ford, the founder of Ford Motor Company who began mass production and made the Ford car affordable for the working class.

While Hill was selling Ford on the interview, Ford was busy selling Hill on the Ford automobile. Hill was so sold on the car that he purchased a Ford for $575 to drive home, the money probably coming from his new bride whose wealthy West Virginia parents gave her a wedding endowment.

On returning to Washington from his interview, Hill founded the Automobile College of Washington to teach people how to sell cars.

Throughout his lifetime, Hill had a love for automobiles. Growing up in a rural area where very few people could afford a car, to Hill and most people the automobile was clearly a sign of wealth. When his first books were published, he paid $25,000 for a Rolls Royce automobile, which was a large sum of money at that time.

Fascinated by the automobile and with his desire to be a writer that started when Hill was a teenager, it seemed natural to use the automobile in articles he wrote.

In Hill's biography, *A Lifetime of Riches*, the author wrote, "like millions of other Americans born into modest or impoverished means," Hill was destined to admire the likes of Thomas Edison, the inventor of the light bulbs, the phonograph and hundreds of other inventions; Andrew Carnegie who like Edison with very little formal education founded U. S. Steel; Henry Ford, founder of the Ford Motor Company, and dozens of other self-made men with a passion that bordered on worship. He would become consumed with interest about people who succeed while others fail. Hill dreamed of meeting these giants like many others to obtain their wisdom that produced their incredible accomplishments.

But unlike most of the other admirers, Napoleon Hill was destined to fulfill his dreams. He would not only meet and impress America's greatest achievers but would spend his entire life gathering their secrets to success and communicating them to the world.

Hill wrote a series of fifteen articles he titled *Billboards on the Road to Success*. The articles in *Napoleon Hill's Road to Success* are exactly as Hill typed them on his old manual typewriter. The articles written more than ninety years ago are as relevant today as when Hill penned them.

I

THE ROAD TO SUCCESS

15 Billboards

BILLBOARD 1

DESIRE AS A DEFINITE AIM IN LIFE

You want to succeed in life!

You want a home and you want a little "nest egg" of money laid away in the bank. Perhaps you want a little automobile of your own and other conveniences with which to enjoy yourself when not engaged in work.

You will have all this, and perhaps much more if you will follow the Road To Success as it is marked off for you in this and other messages that will follow.

The Road to Success has been discovered. It has been surveyed and signboards have been placed along the way. These signboards tell you just what to do. There are fifteen of these signboards and if you will read these messages and do what they tell you, nothing can stop you from succeeding.

These fifteen signboards were thought out by a man who is now very successful. He owns his own home. He owns his own automobile. He has a good-sized bank account. He has a wife and several happy children. He is successful and happy himself. He had no one to help him and no advantages which you do not have, for he started out as a humble laborer in the coal mines not long ago.

This man succeeded, just as you may now succeed, by observing these fifteen signboards on the Road To Success.

The first one of these signboards is called:

A Definite Aim In Life!

Before another sun sets you must decide what *your definite aim in life* is going to be. After you have decided you must write out your definite aim in clear, simple words. You must describe it so clearly that anyone would know what it is after reading your description of it.

Here is how you go about describing your definite aim:

For example, suppose that your aim is to be the owner of a home, an automobile, a nice bank account, and, an income sufficient to give you time for rest and pleasure; you would state your aim in writing in these words:

> "My definite aim in life is to own a home, an automobile and a nice little bank account, and, to have an income sufficient to give me time for rest, recreation and pleasure. *In return for these joys of life I will render the best service at my command, and I will so conduct myself that the purchaser of my services will be satisfied with what I deliver him. To be sure that my employer will always be satisfied with my services I will always endeavor to deliver the best I have regardless of the pay I receive, because my common sense tells me that this habit will make me a very desirable employee and bring me the top-notch price that is paid for the sort of services I am rendering. I will sign my name to this definite aim and read it over every night just before I go to sleep, for twelve consecutive nights.*
>
> (Signed)..

The psychologists claim that any person who writes out a definite aim in words similar to the foregoing, and faithfully observes the habit of reading it every night for twelve nights, just before going to sleep, will be sure to see that aim is fulfilled.

Remember this definite aim is the first step on The Road To Success, and remember, also, that the man who named these signboards started in very humble work, as a laborer in the coal mines, with practically no education, and quickly climbed to success. You can do the same if you will follow the directions in these messages.

Almost from the very day that you write out your definite aim you will notice that things will begin to come your way. You will notice that your fellow-workmen will be more considerate of you. You will notice that your employer will take notice of your work and greet you with a smile such as you never saw before. Unseen forces will come to your rescue and you will begin to sweep on to success as though an army of friendly people was secretly following in your footsteps and helping you in all that you do.

You will also notice that you will become more friendly toward your fellow workers and your employer. You will become more patient with all of your friends and they will begin to like you more and more, until finally you will have no enemies. Everybody will begin to be friendly toward you and these friends will help you achieve success.

This is a promise of one who has tried the plan and found that it worked!

Do not question that it will work as well for you. Follow the instructions laid down in this and the bulletins that will follow and one year from the day that this bulletin came into your hands people who know you will marvel at your personality and you will find yourself an attractive person whom all will like. You will find, also, that all who know you will go out of their way to throw opportunity your way just because they like you.

Your World Is Determined By Your Dominant Desire

This is the hidden secret that unconsciously determines attention. "As a man thinketh in his heart so is he." Notice that phrase "in his heart" or as Hamlet once put it in his "heart of hearts." The Hebrew writers, who in the scripture used the word "heart" as the symbol of man's emotional nature, may have been totally ignorant of modern psychology, yet, as John

Herman Randall points out in his "Culture of Personality," they grasped the great psychological truth that all thought springs from primary feelings or emotions. Personality considered as the self conscious unity of reason, affection and will, finds self expression in a creative process that begins first in an impulse or feeling, passes to thought and completes itself in an act of will. In the last analysis our world is determined by our dominant desires. Personality is the development of desire.

As a man's dominant desire, then so becomes the world of his personality. Or to put it simply; as a man's dominant desire so he becomes. All men in the sense of desire pray. The prodigal's dominant desire was "Give me my portion." Peary said that for twenty-four years, asleep or awake, the one dream and purpose of his life was to find the North Pole. Edison and the incandescent, Stevenson and the locomotive, Fulton and the steamboat, Napoleon and the mastery of Europe, Joan d'Arc and the salvation of France, Paul and the spread of Christianity were the answers of dominant, all controlling desire. Such prayers may be false or true, but prayer is a boomerang. This warns us to keep dominant desire pure and unselfish, in attunement with God's will.

Know a man's fixed desires and you can cast a horoscope as to what he will become. Show me the pictures a man hangs on his walls—the books he has in his library, the movies he goes to see, the sort of friends he gathers about his fireside, and I will tell you the sort of prayers he makes, for these walls of his imagination, the sort of things he writes on the fleshly tablet of his heart, the sort of conversation he holds in his dreams, the thought-world that is controlling his subconscious mind.

If your World is determined by your dominant desire the only way to create a beautiful world, is to think, as Ralph Waldo Trine would say, "in tune with the Infinite;" to think as the great Kepler said, "God's thoughts after him," to think, as the Master himself put it in harmony with the Divine Will—"Thy will be done."

There is only one way to do this. You must practice the

presence of God. The Master pointed that way, when he gave the formula, "Enter your closet, shut the door, and pray in the silence." The psychologist in-all effective thinking. The psychologist and the mystic both agree on the same method to induce the psychological moment, to connect at the throne of God. We are not only what we think in our hearts, but also what we pray in our hearts. Prayer brings us into touch with universal consciousness, the mystic love energy of all being, the eternal God, our Heavenly Father.

We need to constantly call ourselves into the Divine Presence. We need to think of prayer less as petition and more as Communion, Creation and Realization. Prayer itself is the greatest asset a man has. It is not that your child needs to say "Now I lay me down to sleep" for fear God will forget him or fail to watch over him during the night. You teach your little boy or girl to pray "Now I lay me down to sleep" that he or she may learn the prayer path to God and come in mature years to identify dominant or fixed desires with God. It works. The Rev. James Higgins told me that until he was 21 he had never seen a Bible, been inside a church or heard a prayer save "Now I lay me", and "Our Father who art in heaven" which he learned at his mother's knee, and had prayed every night and morning of his life from his earliest recollection. The first public prayer he heard resulted in his conversion and later consecration to the Christian Ministry. A Springfield College student said to me, "Mrs. McCollum's lectures on Applied Psychology have enabled me to realize that my mother's religion as scientific, and that thrills me." It is a wise mother who teaches her child to pray.

Prayer then–real prayer–is dominant desire God-ward, and we are what our prayers make us.

"Prayer is the soul's sincere desire
Uttered or unexpressed
The motion of a hidden fire
That trembles on the breast."

Put your prayer life to pushing, not for God to perform some miracle for you, but to give you the creative energy, that you may perform the miracles for the glory of a better humanity.

Ask God every morning for health, happiness and success with your appointed task. Go forward conscious of his energizing. Expect fulfillment. Accept nothing less. The Godlike spirit can do the Godlike thing. Concentration and Prayer become your greatest asset in creating an efficient personality for human service.

The verse of Clinto Scollard puts it in a cameo.

"Let us put by some hour of every day
For holy things–whether it be when dawn
Peers through the window pane, or when the moon
Flames like a burnished topaz in the vault,
Or when the thrush pours in the ear of eve
Its plaintive melody; some little hour
Wherein to hold rapt converse with the soul
From sordidness and self a sanctuary
Swept by the winnowing of unseen wings
And touched by the White Light Ineffable."

Some twenty years ago a Southern author wrote a book called "Up From Slavery." The man who wrote the book has now passed beyond the Great Divide, but his handiwork stands at Tuskegee, Alabama, in the shape of a monument that will keep his name alive for many generations to come.

The name of the man is Booker T. Washington.

The monument is the Industrial School that he established for the people of his race; a school that teaches its students the honor and glory of learning to work.

This writer has just read "Up From Slavery" for the first time, thanks to Mr. Lincoln Tyler, an eminent New York attorney.

We feel ashamed for not having read it many years ago, because it is a book that every young man and woman ought to read early in life.

If you become discouraged now and then, go to the Library and read this book. It will show you real cause for discouragement.

Booker T. Washington was born a slave. He did not even know who his father was. After the slaves were set free he felt a burning *desire* to educate himself. The word *desire* is printed in italics because this word has an important meaning as it is used in this particular instance.

Washington heard of the school for colored people at Hampton, Virginia. Without funds to pay his way, or to pay for his traveling expenses, he set out, from his little shanty in West Virginia, to walk to Hampton.

In Richmond, Virginia, he stopped for a few days to work as a laborer on a boat that was unloading. His "hotel" was a board sidewalk, and his bed was the cold mother earth. He saved every cent received from his labor on the boat, with the exception of a few cents a day he spent for coarse food. All night long he could hear the "tramp, tramp, tramp" of footsteps on the sidewalk above him, from which we judge that his quarters were none too pleasant.

But he had a burning *desire* to give himself an education, and when men have this sort of a desire for anything, no matter what may be the color of their skin, or the size of their pocket books, they usually get it before they stop.

When the work on the boat was finished Washington turned his face "Hamptonward" once more. Arriving there he had but fifty cents in capital. They looked him over, heard his story, but did not indicate whether or not he might enter as a student.

Finally, the woman in charge of the school gave him an entrance examination. It was quite unlike the test at Harvard, or Princeton, or Yale, but nevertheless it was a test. She asked him to step inside and clean a certain room.

Washington went to the task with the determination to do a good job, for he had a burning *desire* to enter that school. He swept the room four times. Then he went over every inch of it with a cleaning rag four times.

The woman came to inspect his work. She took her handkerchief and searched for a speck of dust, but the search was in vain. No dust was to be found. She said to the young colored lad, "I guess you'll do to enter this school."

Before Booker T. Washington died he had raised himself to such a position of honor that he rubbed elbows with kings and potentates, the "rubbing" being always at their invitation. He sought no prestige. He craved no "equal rights" of a social nature with the whites.

As a public speaker he swept his audiences before him. His style was that of simplicity. He used no big words. He did not "four-flush." He acted naturally always. His simple, direct, straight-forward manner made a place for him in the hearts of both his own people and the white people of the United States and many other countries.

A lesson, here, for all who seek glory and honor in any calling.

Washington taught his people to give more time to learning how to lay bricks and build houses and raise cotton than to the study of dead languages or literature. He understood the real meaning of the word "educate." He knew that education means developing from within; learning to render a needed service; learning how to get all that was needed without interfering with the rights of others.

Tuskegee, Alabama, is now one of the most progressive of cities. It is known for the achievement of the school that Washington founded, not only all over America, but practically all over the world. The school property, within itself, constitutes a splendid city.

Booker T. Washington made one statement in his "Up From Slavery" that stood out like a bright star in the mind of this writer. He said that a man's success should be judged, not by what he had achieved, but by "the obstacles he has overcome."

How true this is. We know a family here in New York City that owns many millions of dollars' worth of the choicest property in the city, but not a single member of that family did anything to earn a cent of that money. The members of the family are considered "successful."

Booker T. Washington, starting as a slave who had never owned enough clothing to cover his body until he was a large boy, mastered obstacles that would cause most of us to throw up our hands and quit. He struggled in the face of two unusually difficult obstacles—race prejudice and poverty.

Yet, in spite of all this handicap he won a place for himself and for his race that many others with less obstacles to overcome might well envy.

He was right! It is not what a man possesses in the way of material wealth that counts; it is what he overcomes in the way of obstacles.

Read the Washington book. Take it away into some quiet corner and do some thinking as you read. Compare Washington's obstacles with some of your own, past or present, that you considered insurmountable. The reading of this book will prove to be a powerful inspiration to you.

To read the book is both educational and interesting. Washington makes one laugh and he makes one cry. He tells of his first hat. Being too poor to buy a "store hat" his mother made one for him out of two pieces of old cloth. When he appeared with it on, the other colored children who had "boughten" hats, laughed and made fun of him. He relates, with no evident feeling of satisfaction, that in later years most of those who laughed at his hat found their way to the penitentiary or were still doing nothing to better themselves or their race.

All who make writing their profession ought to read "Up From Slavery." It is written in a style that makes one know that no facts are being withheld. Washington makes no attempt to shield either himself or his race, or to give prominence or undue credit to either. Logic runs all the way through it. Truth is evident on every page. Read it.

Now is the time to take inventory of your past experiences and find out what you have learned that is of use to you, and what you wish to accomplish while your candle is still burning.

Ask yourself these questions and insist on answers:

What have I learned from my failures and mistakes that will be of service to me in the future? What have I done to entitle me to a higher position in life? What have I done to make the world a better place? What is education, and how can I educate myself? Does it profit me to strike back at those who have injured me? How can I find happiness? How can I succeed? What is success? Lastly, what main achievement do I wish to attain before I finally lay down the tools with which I am tinkering and pass over the Great Divide? What is my definite aim in life?

Write out your answers to all of these questions and think before you write. The result may startle you, because these questions, if carefully answered, will cause you to do more constructive thinking than the average person does in a whole lifetime.

Do much thinking before you answer the last question. Find out what it really is that you want in life. Then find out if it is apt to bring you happiness after you get it.

The one object in life that transcends all others is that of finding happiness. Examine yourself and you will find that all of your motives lead, finally, in search of happiness. You want money so you can buy independence and happiness. You want a home and luxuries that you may be happy.

And, in your search for answers to these questions you are sure to find that happiness–the genuine brand that satisfies and endures–comes only by giving it to others. By this route you can find it without money and without price. The minute you deliver it to others, through helpful service, you have it yourself, in abundance.

May it not be well if, in your decision as to your definite aim in life, you include happiness?

In every normal mind a sleeping genius lies, waiting for the gentle touch of strong **desire** to arouse it and put it into action!

Listen, you sorrow-laden brothers who are groping for the pathway which leads out of the darkness of failure into the light of achievement–there is hope for you.

It makes no difference how many are the failures you have undergone or how low you may have fallen, you can get on your feet again! The person who said that opportunity never knocks but once was woefully mistaken. Opportunity stands at your door day and night. True, she does not hammer at your door or try to break in the panels, but she is none the less there.

What if you have undergone failure after failure? Every failure is but a blessing in disguise–a blessing that has tempered your mental and prepared you for the next test! If you have never undergone failure you are to be pitied for you have missed one of Nature's great processes of true education.

What if you have erred in the past? Who of us has not done the same? Find the person who has never erred and you will find also a person who has never done anything worth mentioning.

The distance from where you now are to the place where you wish to be is but a hop, skip and jump! Possibly you have become a victim of habit and, like many another, you have become enmeshed in a mediocre life-work. Take courage–there is a way out! Perhaps fortune has passed you by and poverty has you within its grip. Take courage–there is a pathway to all that you can use intelligently and for your own good, and the chart of that pathway is so simple that we seriously doubt that you will make use of it. If you do, however, you are sure to be rewarded.

The Golden Rule should be adopted as the business slogan of every business concern and professional man in America, and printed as such on every letterhead.

The forerunner to all human accomplishment is **desire!** So powerful is the human mind that it can produce the wealth you desire, the position you covet, the friendship you need, the qualities which are necessary for achievement in any worthwhile undertaking.

There is a difference between "wish" and "desire," in the sense that we are here referring to it. A wish is merely the seed or germ of the thing wished for, while strong "**desire**" is the germ of the thing desired, plus the necessary fertile soil, the sunshine and the rain for its development and growth.

Strong **desire** is the mysterious force which arouses that sleeping genius reposing in the human brain and puts it to work in earnest. Desire is the spark which bursts forth into a flame in the boiler of human effort and generates the steam with which to produce **action!**

Life is made up of one long facing of decisions—of deciding promptly or letting the opportunity pass. Doing or failing to do may equally affect us for good or for ill. Character is built up by the influence on us of the endless chain of decisions we are called upon to make so long as life is in us.

Many and varied are the influences which arouse **desire** and put it to work. Sometimes the death of a friend or relative will do it, while at other times financial reverses will have the right effect. Disappointment, sorrow and adversities of every nature serve to arouse the human mind and cause it to function through new channels. When you come to understand that failure is only a temporary condition which arouses you to greater action you will see, as plainly as you can see the sky on a clear day, that failure is a blessing in disguise. And, when you come to look upon adversity and failure in this light you will begin to come into the greatest power on the face of this earth. You will then actually begin to make capital out of failure instead of allowing it to drag you down.

There is a happy day coming in your life! It is going to arrive when you discover that whatever you aspire to accomplish depends, not upon others, but upon **you!** The arrival of this new day will be preceded by your discovery of the strength of **desire!**

Start in now, right today, to create a strong and irrepressible desire for the station in life which you wish to attain. Make that desire so full and complete that it will absorb most of your thought. Dwell upon it by day and dream about it by night. Keep your mind focused on it during every spare moment. Write it out on paper and place it where you can see it at all times. Concentrate your every effort toward its realization, and lo! As if in response to the touch of a magic wand, it will materialize itself for you.

BILLBOARD 2

SELF-CONFIDENCE

The second signboard on the Road to Success is Self-Confidence.

To be sure of success you must believe in yourself. You cannot believe in yourself unless others believe in you also, and you cannot get others to believe in you unless you deserve it.

If every person whom you met today would tell you that you look sick you would have to have a doctor before night. If the next three people you speak to today should tell you that you look sick you would begin to feel sick.

On the other hand, if every person you see toady should tell you what a likeable person you are it would influence you to believe in yourself. If your employer should compliment you each day and tell you what fine work you are doing it would cause you to believe in yourself. If your fellow-workmen should tell you each day that you are doing better work this would make you have greater confidence in yourself.

We all need someone to believe in us and to encourage us.

It has been said by those who know, that a man's wife can lead him on to success by sending him away to his work each day with a glad smile and a word of encouragement. The man who created these signboards on the Road to Success gives much off the credit for his success to his wife. She sent him away to his work each day with this encouraging thought:

"You Are Going to Do Good Work Today!"

She never nagged at him. She never criticized him. She never scolded if he was late. She always told him what a bright man she thought he was. One day she did a very unusual thing—she wrote out a creed for her husband to sign and hang in front of him where he could see it all day long while at his work. This is a copy of the creed:

> *"I believe in myself. I believe in those who work with me. I believe in my employer. I believe in my friends. I believe in my family. I believe that God will lend me everything I need with which to succeed if I do my best to earn it through faithful, efficient and honest service. I believe in prayer and I will never close my eyes in sleep without praying for Divine guidance to the end that I will be patient with other people and tolerant with those who do not think as I do. I believe that success is the result of intelligent effort and does not depend upon luck, sharp practices or double-crossing friends, fellow-workmen or my employer. I believe that I will get out of life exactly what I put into it, therefore I will be careful to conduct myself toward others as I would be willing to have them act toward me. I will not slander those whom I do not like, I will not slight my work no matter what I may see others doing. I will render the best service that is in me because I have pledged myself to succeed in life and I know that success is always the result of conscientious effort. Finally, I will forgive those who offend me because I realize that I will sometimes offend others and I will need their forgiveness."*
>
> (Signed)..

Do you wonder why this young man who started as a laborer in the coal mines has risen to success and wealth when you read the creed that he signed and did his best to live up to?

This is a good creed for you to sign and place before you at your work, where you can see it each day, and, where others can see it. You may find it hard to live up to this creed at first, but, everything worth having costs a price of some sort. The price of Self-Confidence is conscientious effort to live up to this creed.

If you are married, show this creed to your life partner. If you are not married show it to someone whom you would like to make your life partner and ask that person to assist you in living up to the creed.

Believe in yourself if you want others to believe in you. Expect success of yourself if you wish others to expect success of you. The world accepts you at pretty much your own valuation, therefore set the value high.

It pays handsomely to believe in yourself, and it pays to develop that sort of personality that causes others to believe in themselves. We know a man who devotes his entire life to helping others build self-confidence. The other day he received notice that a successful business man had included him in his will for a large bequest. In explanation the donor said: "Reading one of your books helped me to become a successful man and I am leaving a part of my wealth to you that you may go right ahead helping others as you have helped me."

Helping others to help themselves pays in more ways than in mere dollars; it pays in happiness. You can be wealthy in money and you can be wealthy in that "something" which money cannot buy and which cannot be measured by a monetary standard if you will develop the art of helping men to help themselves. Believe in yourself first. This is the first requisite for all worthwhile attainments.

"YOU"

You are the most important person in the whole world. In you are all of the elements of a successful man. You have within you all the latent forces that will lift you to your desires—in success and happiness. This article will help you to realize more and more that you are a man of worth—and the most important person in the world.

Whatever you desire you can have—for in the development of your ability your desires will frame themselves within measurable size. And with a correct understanding of your desires will come a realization of your power to secure them.

Honors and riches and power might come to you by accident, unearned and uninvited, but they will not serve you, and you will lose them again unless you are prepared to receive them and to use them aright.

The whole of a man's power lies within himself, and a man's first duty is to himself. In carrying out that duty faithfully, you cannot fail to leave your impress on the society in which you move, you cannot fail to raise the standard of your environment, and to dignify all your surroundings.

You may be only one of hundreds or thousands all working in a great business house. Your immediate duties may seem monotonous and trivial. There is no apparent incentive for enthusiasm or personal pride. Be yourself and show yourself. Your job will always be what you want it to be–it will always be what you deserve. It is not your job, it is not your pay, or your conditions, or your prospects–it is YOU.

Believe in your own ability to do big things. Only by having faith in yourself can you compel others to have faith in you.

Whatever you are called upon to do should receive your whole-hearted attention and interest; your maximum ability. Do it in such a way that those above you will take notice. You can compel them to notice if only your actions have enough vigor and common sense. It all depends upon You.

To become despondent about your lot in life is but to belittle yourself without helping yourself. To be determined on better things, and ready and anxious to work for better things, will surely bring its reward.

There is no necessity to wait for other people to die before you get promoted. You can wait if you wish, but there is no need for it. You are just wearying and wearing yourself in the waiting. You alone are responsible. No firm would have an institution of promotion by seniority if every man and woman, boy or girl, exerted themselves more, had a bigger opinion of themselves, and worked according to that opinion. In gauging your own importance, do not allow yourself to float in a sea of superlative egotism. Do not let your head swell. A proper estimate of one's self must include credit for retaining control.

When you realize your importance you will keep control of it, so that you may apply your power in a sensible and cool way. You are bigger than you think you are. Act up to this.

Do your present work better than anybody at your age or experience has ever done it before. Thus you show yourself fit for still higher duties. These higher duties will come, and as you tackle them in the same forward spirit, a further advancement will be inevitable. And so you will go on, and on. Everything lies with yourself. Nothing can keep you down if only you decide that you will move up.

Most truly great men started in a small way–lower down the scale than you, whatever your present position may be. But they found themselves, they knew themselves, they recognized the power of the man who says, "I will." Opportunities will not come to you unless you have an opinion of yourself big enough to grasp them.

Be determined to better the work you are doing. Show how you can produce more at less cost of mental and physical energy.

You were not born to remain always in your present station. There is room for you higher up if you are ready to climb to it. There is pleasure in the climbing, too. Work is a pleasure if we make it so. Drudgery has no meaning for the boy or man who has an aim in life.

A better job than the one you are doing now is waiting for you. You cannot get it by asking for it, and no matter how or when you get it, you must fill it well, and so prepare for another. The world is calling for persons who think well of themselves, sufficiently well to dignify themselves by doing each task efficiently and with a result for pride. There is a better position waiting for you, but you must show yourself worthy of it by filling your present job so full that your ability shows itself to be running over. Somebody will see it, and use it.

Whatever is worth having is worth working for. Don't fume

or fret at the success of some other person. Use your time for your own ends; apply it to your immediate task and do not pay too much attention to the result–it will come. It is inevitable. It is the law.

Treat yourself as a man of worth. Demand much of yourself. Be your own hardest taskmaster.

For you the greatest thing is yourself. Use yourself right; think well of yourself; work hard for yourself. Others will benefit in the process–do not deny them of this. Rest assured that your own reward is as certain as the work you do to secure it.

Don't pity yourself. Don't lessen your own value in your own eyes. Have confidence in yourself.

You are the most important person in the world. You can be what you want to be. Nobody can do so much for you as you can do for yourself. Everything lies with You.

Self-Confidence

Our doubts are traitors, and make us lose
the good we oft might win by fearing to attempt.
–SHAKESPEARE

Lincoln started in a log hut and stopped in the White House–because he believed in himself. Napoleon began as a poor Corsican and brought half of Europe to his feet–because he believed in himself. Henry Ford started as a poor farmer lad and put more wheels into motion than any other man on earth–because he believed in himself. Rockefeller started as a poor bookkeeper and became the world's richest man–because he believed in himself. They took that which they wished because they had confidence in their own ability. Now, the question is, WHY DO YOU NOT DECIDE WHAT YOU WANT, THEN GO OUT AND TAKE IT?

BILLBOARD 3

INITIATIVE

The third signboard on the Road to Success is *Initiative!*

In plain words, *Initiative* means that you will do the thing that you ought to do without someone else telling you to do it.

The man who created these signboards on the Road to Success was raised down in the mountains of Wise, Virginia. He had but little schooling. He had no home and but few friends when he went to work as a water boy in the mines.

Carrying water did not keep him busy, so he put in his odd time helping drivers unhitch their mules at the coal tipple. One day the owner of the mines came along and saw this lad helping the drivers do their work. The owner stopped the lad and asked who had told him to do this extra work.

The boy replied: "No one told me to do it, but I have some extra time and I thought no one would care if I put it to good use by helping the drivers with their work."

The owner of the mines started to walk away. He turned suddenly to this lad and said: "You come to my office this evening after you quit work." The lad was scared because he thought this meant that he would lose his job for doing something he had not been told to do. With fear and trembling he marched into the owner's office that evening.

The mine owner saw he was scared, so he quickly assured him that he need not be afraid. He asked the lad to have a seat, then he said to him:

"My boy, do you know that we have several hundred men working at this plant and we have more than a score of foremen whose work is to see that these men do what they are told to do and do it right. Out of all these hundreds of men you are the first one I have had to call to my office on account of having helped the other fellow do his work without being told to do so. You have that rare quality called *Initiative,* and if you will keep on using it you can someday be in any position around here that you want."

The mine owner then turned to his work and the boy got up and slipped out of the office. This was one of the happiest moments of his life. He had gone to the office expecting to be "fired" and he had actually been complimented instead.

Five years later this boy was appointed General Manager of that same coal mine, with more than a thousand men under his direction. At that time he was the youngest General Manager of a coal mine in the United States. The men all liked him because they had confidence in him. Over the pay-window there was a great big sign that read as follows:

TO MY FELLOW-WORKERS

Five years ago the General Manager of this plant was working as a water boy at wages of fifty cents a day.

One day the owner of the mines caught this water boy helping the drivers unhitch their mules at Tipple Number Three.

He was not paid to do this extra work. No one asked him to do it. He did it because he wanted to lend a helping hand and lighten the burden of the drivers.

Such initiative is a valuable part of any man's tool-kit. Every man who draws his pay at this window has the same opportunity to advance to a more responsible position than this water boy had, and he can do it in exactly the same manner.

No man on these works is required to do a part of another fellow's work, but there is nothing to stop him from doing so if he chooses, and, if any man shows as much initiative as this water boy displayed, he can eventually have one of the best jobs on these works because no one can stop him.

From today on you should take advantage of the opportunities that come to the person who uses initiative, because this is one of the most important signboards on the Road to Success.

Your instructions in connection with this signboard on *Initiative* are simple and easily followed. For the next ten days make it your business to use *Initiative* by doing at least one thing each day that you are not told to do in connection with your work. Say nothing to anyone about what you are doing, but keep your own counsel and follow these instructions. If your work is of such a nature that you cannot perform work that you are not told to perform, then speed up a bit and perform more work and better work than you have been performing in the same length of time. Keep this up for ten days and by that time you will attract attention of your employer. You will also see, by the end of the ten days, that it will pay you to use *Initiative* the remainder of your life, because *Initiative* leads to greater responsibility, to a bigger pay envelope and helps you to get whatever you have decided upon as your *definite aim in life.*

Initiative

The world bestows its big prizes, both in money and honors, for one thing, and that is *Initiative.*

What is *Initiative?* I'll tell you: It is doing the right thing without being told.

But next to doing the right thing without being told is to do it when you are told once. That is to say, carry the message to Garcia; those who can carry a message get high honors, but their pay is not always in proportion.

Next, there are those who never do a thing until they are told twice; such get no honors and small pay.

Next, there are those who do the right thing only when necessity kicks them from behind, and these get indifference instead of honors, and a pittance for pay.

This kind spend most of the time polishing a bench with a hard luck story.

Then, still lower down in the scale than this we have the fellow who will not do the right thing even when someone goes along to show him how and stays to see that he does it; he is always out of a job, and receives the contempt he deserves, unless he has a rich Pa, in which case destiny patiently waits around the corner with a stuffed club.

To which class do *you* belong?

–ELBERT HUBBARD

BILLBOARD 4

IMAGINATION

The fourth signboard on the Road to Success is *Imagination!*

Every successful person must use *imagination.* You do not have to be well educated before you can use your imagination. When you use imagination you simply build new plans out of old ideas, very much as one might build a new house out of old brick.

One day a young man was walking along in a line of people with a tray in his hands, getting ready to help himself to his dinner in a cafeteria. As he stood in line his *imagination* began to work. He thought to himself, "Why wouldn't it be a good idea to open a self-help grocery store, where people can come in, fill their baskets with whatever they want, and pay at the door as they go out."

He rented a small store and put his self-help grocery store idea to work. Now he has stores in dozens of towns and cities. His idea has made him a wealthy man. His self-help grocery stores save time and they save money for those who trade there.

Look around and see if you cannot make *your imagination* work for you. If you can do your work in less time and do it as well, you have an idea that is valuable. If you see a way to help someone else do his work in less time you also have an idea that is valuable. Anything that will save time and labor is worth money. Remember this and be on the lookout all the time for a plan or an idea that will save you time, because this plan will help you on the road to success.

Down in the Southern States they raise cotton. They used to

throw the cotton seeds away or dump them out in big piles. These seeds were good for nothing. It cost money to haul them away.

One day a young man came along and saw those big piles of cotton seeds. He picked up a handful and crushed one of them between his teeth. He found that it was full of rich oil.

He got a tin pan full of the seeds and crushed them with a hammer. He poured the crushed seeds into a bag and squeezed the oil out of them. He found that the oil was good for many things. He also found that the seeds were good for food for cattle after the oil was squeezed out.

This young man had used his *imagination.* He discovered that the seeds which the cotton growers were throwing away were the most valuable part of their crops. He began to buy these seeds and make oil and feed for cattle out of them. His discovery made him a very wealthy man.

Now they save all the cotton seeds. This young man's *imagination* was worth millions of dollars a year.

Anybody who finds out how to save anything of value that is going to waste is putting his *imagination* to good use. Perhaps there is an opportunity for *you* to use your *imagination* by stopping some leak or saving time for someone where you work. If you can find this opportunity it will help you on the Road to Success.

Out on the Pacific coast, in California, a city had been built as close to the sea as they could build it. The city grew until it covered all the level land they had.

On one side there was a big steep hill that overlooked the ocean. They could not build houses on this hill because it was too steep. At the foot of the hill the ground was level, but it was covered with back water from the ocean most of the time. It was too wet for building purposes.

No one thought this ground was worth much because no houses could be built on it.

One day a man with *imagination* came along. He walked up on top of the steep hill and looked down at the ground that was covered with back water. Then his *imagination* began to work. He had trained it to work for him. He saw what anyone else living in that city could have seen if he had used his *imagination.*

He went to the owner of the low, water-covered ground and bought it for a small sum. Then he went to the owner of the steep hill and brought it for a small sum. He then bought some dynamite and blew the steep hill down into the swamp and filled it up. This turned the swamp into beautiful lots. It also left a level place where the hill had stood and he sold it for building lots. This man with *imagination* made a fortune in a few months' time by removing the dirt from the steep hill down into the low ground where it was needed.

Take a look around the place where you work. If you will use your *imagination* you will see some change that could be made that will save time or labor. You will find some way to do *your work* in less time, or you will see some way to do more work in the same time. This will be worth money to your employer and to you.

No man can become a power in his community or achieve enduring success until he becomes big enough to blame himself with his mistakes and failures.

Imagination is one of the most important subjects in this course of lessons on finding the Road to Success!

If you will use your *imagination* in your work you will be bound to get ahead.

Just a little over three hundred years ago a poor sailor boy used his *imagination* and found a new country. That was the most profitable use of *imagination* ever recorded in the history of the world.

That sailor's name was Christopher Columbus!

From the shores of Spain he looked out into the Atlantic Ocean and "imagined" that there must be land on the other side. He got three small sailing boats together and started to look for that land. He did not find it the first day nor the first week nor the first month, but he kept on sailing.

He finally sailed his little boats to this country. As a result of Columbus' *imagination* we now have the best, the freest and the richest country in the world. We have a country where everyone can own a home. We have a country where everyone has a chance to work who wants to work. We have a country where everyone may believe as he pleases and worship God in his own way. No such freedom as this was possible where Columbus came from, when he set out to find America.

Your freedom in this great American country was made possible because Columbus used his *imagination.* There may be no more big countries like this to discover through your *imagination,* but there are plenty of chances for you to help make this still a better country.

Nearly two thousand years ago a little child was born in the old country. Its parents were so poor that they had no home and the child was born in a stable.

This child had but little schooling. It had no wealthy parents and but few friends. It had but little freedom, as men had less freedom in those days then we have now.

At the age of twelve this child began to use its *imagination.* This twelve-year-old boy saw that men were not kind to one another. He saw the need of more kindness and more freedom in the world. He formed a little union of men; perhaps the first union in the world. This union had but twelve members.

This boy grew into manhood. He became a great preacher. His preaching was simple and easily understood, just as all great things are simple and easily understood. This great preacher devoted his entire life to telling men that the only thing worthwhile in this world was happiness. He told them that they could *get* happiness only by *giving* it to others.

Some ignorant men caught this great preacher and hung him on a cross until he died, but they did not kill his message. His message was sound. It was based on *truth* and *justice,* and nothing can stop a message that is based on justice to all men. This great preacher now has millions of believers in His message. Perhaps *you* are one of them. If you are, you remember His greatest sermon. It was called the Sermon on the Mount, and it may be found in the book of Matthew, in the Holy Bible.

In that sermon this great preacher told us to "Do unto others as we would have them do unto us." That is a good rule to follow. It has lived for two thousand years and no one has yet violated it without coming to grief.

When you think of this great preacher, Jesus Christ, remember that he devoted his entire life to showing men and women that the only thing in this world worth having is happiness, and, that we can *get* happiness only by *giving* it to others.

One day a poor young lad started down the Mississippi River on a flat boat. This young fellow was born in a log hut that had nothing but dirt for a floor.

In New Orleans he saw white men selling colored men and women as slaves. His *imagination* began to work. It did not look right to him for colored men and women to be sold as slaves.

His *imagination* told him that it was wrong to sell men and women in a free country like this. Many years passed by. This young country lad became a man. He read in his Bible about that great preacher who was born in a stable. He remembered what that preacher said about "doing unto others as you would have them do unto you."

It did not seem to him that slave-selling was practicing what Jesus Christ taught. He made up his mind to stop slave-selling in America. Finally this man's chance came. The people of America made him their President. Then he put a stop to selling colored people into slavery. This man Lincoln set the rest of us a good example to follow. He gave his life to keep this country the freest place on earth.

Lincoln believed in justice for all. He believed we should be honest and truthful with each other. He believed that we should practice the Golden Rule in the shops and stores and everywhere that men meet each other. We have never had a better

President than Lincoln. He believed that everyone in America had a right to freedom. He believed that a man had a right to the fruits of his own labor, no matter whether he was white or black. He believed that everyone had a right to protection in this great country as long as he behaved himself.

Use *your* imagination and perhaps you will do something that will place your name among the immortals who have risen above mediocrity.

BILLBOARD 5

ENTHUSIASM

The fifth signboard on the Road to Success is *enthusiasm!*

Everyone likes a person who is enthusiastic and cheerful. *Enthusiasm* will make your work seem lighter. It will make your hours seem shorter.

Enthusiasm is "catching." When one person gets it everyone around that person also gets it. No salesman could make a success selling goods without being enthusiastic over what he was selling.

Out in the Arizona state prison is a young man who was sent there for "life." Before he went to prison he was an ill-tempered fellow who never was enthusiastic over his work. He was always in trouble and never succeeded at anything. When they locked him up for life he soon saw that the prison was going to be a very lonesome place for a man who had no *enthusiasm,* so he started in to pretend that he was enthusiastic over his work. He went at his work with a smile on his face and worked as hard as if they had been paying him for it. He soon learned to like the game of "*Enthusiasm*" that he was playing. This attracted the attention of the prison officials and they allowed him more liberties. He turned his attention to writing during his idle moments. He began to practice writing sales letters. He soon became so efficient at this that he attracted attention of business people who bought his letters.

His letters were interesting because he put *enthusiasm* into writing them. The prison officials allowed him still more liberty until today he is making a good income from his writing. This ought to make some of us who are not in prison think about *enthusiasm.* Some day this prisoner will be pardoned, and he will go out into the world and succeed in a big way. Become enthusiastic over your work and you will not only enjoy it more, but you can soon make more money.

Not so many years ago Edwin C. Barnes rode a freight car into Orange, New Jersey. He went there to ask Thomas A. Edison for a job.

He got the job, but it did not pay well at the start. The work was not easy, but Mr. Barnes made up his mind that he was going to work for Mr. Edison, no matter what sort of a job he had to take to start with.

Mr. Edison is a very smart man. He wanted to test Mr. Barnes out, so he gave him a hard job at low wages, to find out how long he would stick to a job and how badly he wanted to work for Mr. Edison.

Mr. Barnes tackled that job with *enthusiasm.* He worked as if he were getting the best wages on the works. He worked with a smile on his face. Everyone around the Edison works began to like him. Although his work was hard and his wages were low he pitched right in and made himself useful.

That has not been so very many years ago. Mr. Barnes is still a young man but he showed so much *enthusiasm* over his work that he was promoted many times. He now has offices of his own in New York, St. Louis and Chicago, where he sells the "Ediphone" dictating machines. He is a wealthy man and owns a beautiful home in Bradentown, Florida.

A big jump for a young fellow who rode into Orange, New Jersey, on a freight car, because he was too poor to buy a railroad ticket. Mr. Barnes' rise to success and fortune is due very largely to his *enthusiasm* over his work. Dislike your work and it will master you, but, become *enthusiastic* over it and you will master it. You can see what would have happened to Mr. Barnes if he had kicked about the hard job and the low wages that Mr. Edison started him out with. He made the best of a hard job and very soon a better job at higher wages came his way.

During the next month do your work as if it were a game you were playing. No matter whether you like your work or not, do it with *enthusiasm,* just as if you did like it.

Remember that a life prisoner in the Arizona state prison found a way to be *enthusiastic* over work that he was forced to do and for which he received no pay. Remember, also, that the prison officials gave him more liberty and took an interest in him because of this *enthusiasm.* You have many advantages over the man who was shut up inside the dark walls of a prison, therefore you will find it much easier to play at this game of *enthusiasm* that he did.

Keep up this game of *enthusiasm* for one month, no matter what you may see others doing. Say nothing to anyone as to why you are doing this. You will get a lot of fun out of this game. You will notice that people will begin to show more interest in you. You will notice that your employer will begin to watch you, but you must keep your own counsel and go right ahead with your game. You must keep the fact in mind that you are on the Road to Success, and the signboards on the road told you to play at the game of *enthusiasm* for one whole month.

You may not know why you are instructed to play at this game of *enthusiasm,* but, you will see long before the end of the month that it paid to follow instructions.

Two hoboes met in a box car one dark and rainy night. One of them had been a salesman whose hours were from 10 A.M. to 4 P.M., and the other one didn't have any money either.

They started to talk about themselves. One of them said to the other: "I used to work for a house that wanted me to put in regular hours. They talked a lot about this *enthusiasm* bunk, but it never made much of a hit with me. I told 'em I would work my way or not at all. They didn't like my way, so I put on my hat and walked out."

The other 'Bo had been a smart fellow in his time, but whiskey and gambling had ruined him. He listened to his pal for a few minutes, then asked this question:

"How is it, Bill, that a fellow who knows as much as you do

about running his employer's business, is riding in a box car instead of a Pullman coach?"

That question was a stunner! Haven't you noticed among the people you have met that the fellow who is a failure usually criticizes the fellow who is succeeding?

You will notice that successful people are too busy *succeeding* to waste any of their time in criticizing their country, their government, their fellow-workers or their employer. You will notice that people who are succeeding are *enthusiastic* over their work, and you never hear them explaining how they lost their jobs.

You will also notice that people who mix *enthusiasm* with their work are always in the best jobs and get the highest pay. You will also notice that the fellow who shows no *enthusiasm* over anything, and is always complaining about his job being too hard and his pay too small, is the first one to be let out when work is slack.

BILLBOARD 6

ACTION

The sixth billboard on the road to success is *action.*

In size the man is about a hundred million times larger than the bee, but in intelligence the bee is about a hundred million times larger than the man.

The man gazes proudly at his handiwork, the great sky-scrapers which blend into distance, and says to himself–"See what a wonderful being I am; see what great buildings I have constructed; see what evolution has done for the human race; see the wealth I have created."

The intelligent little bee, standing guard at the entrance to its hive, hears the man boasting and replies–"Yes, it is true you have made wonderful changes on the earth's surface; you have turned dirt into sky-scrapers; you have built powerful locomotives; you have mastered the air and you have measured the distance to the stars; but one thing you have not done, in spite of all your achievement, is to discover the possibilities within that head of yours. Another thing you have not discovered is the community spirit! You have yet to find out that there is something in the world to work for which is greater than your individual welfare.

"You work for the selfish end of taking away from your fellow-workers that which they have acquired. You have not yet discovered the 'hive spirit' which we little bees observe. We store honey for the good of the hive, while you store up money with which to strangle your fellow-worker and control him for your individual gain."

What a wonderful little insect!

What a wonderful lesson he can teach us if we will only watch him, analyze his habits, and think!

The bee is the only living thing on earth that can control and determine sex before birth!

Man, in all of his wisdom, with all of his advancement, with all of his knowledge of biology and physiology can neither predetermine nor control sex!

The little honey-bee can control sex!

Go out and buy a book on bees and study up on them. Go out to the hive, lie down in front of it and watch the bee at his work. He is an interesting little insect, from which you can learn much that will be of value to you.

There are three kinds of bees in every hive. One is the Queen, which is the mother or female bee. She lays the eggs and keeps the race alive. That is her sole duty. Then, there is the drone, or the male bee. His sole function is to fertilize the eggs which the female lays. Then, there are the workers–those little, intelligent fellows who gather the honey from the flowers and store it up for the use of the whole hive. They are neither male nor female.

There is only one female or Queen bee in each hive. If a boy throws a rock into the hive and kills the Queen, or if she dies from any other cause, the other bees, *through a process known only to the bee,* immediately fertilize an egg that will hatch out another Queen bee in a very short time.

After the male bee has performed the function for which Nature created him, the workers jump on him and sting him to death. There is a decree in "beedom" that all who do not work must get out! Not a bad idea.

You will notice that most of the bees in every hive are workers! This is no mere accident upon the part of Nature. She has provided the bees with a method of producing drones, females and workers in whatever proportion they may determine.

But the greatest lesson that man can learn from the bee is

that of unselfishness!

Bees work with the community spirit. They recognize something higher than the individual himself. They work for their fellow-bees and not against them.

They store up honey in a common storehouse, from which the whole hive may eat.

Imagine selfish, stingy, conceited man doing likewise! Imagine man sharing the product of his labors with his fellowmen unless by so doing he *gets* more than he *gives!*

Man has advanced far beyond the bee, in some respects, but may it not be possible that he kicked out of the harness and strayed away from Nature's plans when he discarded the "community spirit" and started in to defeat and defraud his fellow-workers out of that which they have accumulated?

We do not profess to know what are Nature's plans, but we strongly suspect that before man can enjoy the blessings which are here and available for him he must overcome the spirit of greed, the tendency to *get* without *giving* and come back to the bee habit of working for the "hive!"

This writer knows beyond the question of doubt that the only real happiness which he enjoys is that which comes from serving his fellowmen, and we doubt not that many another has discovered this same truth.

After you have looked everywhere else for the cause of your unhappiness, turn the spotlight on your own heart, examine the thoughts in which you have been indulging, and you may find it.

The Golden Rule lays down a principle which is more than a mere preachment. It bids you go out and get whatever you wish by first giving.

We do not know whether man got the concept laid down in the Golden Rule from the busy little bee, or whether the bee got the idea for his "hive spirit" from the Golden Rule, but we do know that the law underlying the Golden Rule Philosophy is as immutable as is the law of gravitation which keeps the planets of the universe in their places.

And whether a man is conscious of this fact or not, his acts toward his fellowmen are coming back to him greatly multiplied. You are constantly attracting to you men and forces which exactly harmonize with your own thoughts and deeds! There is no escape from this. It is in accordance with a law of the universe.

In all this strife, in all this chaotic turmoil which is going on between so-called "capital" and "labor," we see a perfect antithesis of the "hive spirit."

What a profitable lesson both sides could learn from the humble little honey-bee!

We repeat that we believe the only real success comes from useful service–service which helps others attain monetary success and happiness. Anything short of this sort of service is not success, but failure!

We believe the human race must develop the "hive spirit" before it can advance higher. On every hand we see the futility of trying to *get* without *giving.* Before we have anything to *give* we must prepare, through practice and labor; we must develop the community spirit.

Our point is more clearly stated in the words of George Harrison Phelps, in his recent little book entitled "Go." This story centers around Ben Hur and his chariot race.

"The great race of the day is almost ended. The charioteers are nearing the last turn to finish in front of the royal stand. Every one leans forward. There is no sound throughout the vast Coliseum save the rush of the flying horses, the thunder of the chariots, the cries of the charioteers.

"The speed is terrific. Ben Hur is driving in second place. They approach the last corner. The leaders pitch forward. Driver and chariot and horses all roll in front of Ben Hur.

"Like a flash he takes a double hold on the reins and, fairly lifting the horses, drives them over the prostrate bodies in his path.

"As he swings into the stretch, Artimidora cries to him from the royal box: 'Those arms–where did you get those arms?' He shouts in answer: *'At the galley's oar! At the galley's oar!'*

"In the hold of a trireme, Ben Hur got those mighty arms that carried him to victory. For years he had slaved at a great oar among the hundred other slaves–half-naked and sweating–the lash at his back.

"'Do the thing and you shall have power,' said Emerson. After Ben Hur's years of herculean toil it was an easy task to lift the horses over the wrecked chariot and drive them to the front.

"All great things are accomplished easily–it is the years, the hours, the moments of preparation that count. Thomas Edison was not twenty minutes, proving the value of the incandescent light–he spent a life time seeking the best filament. Abraham Lincoln wrote the greatest speech ever made in the English language–the Gettysburg address–on the back of an envelope, an hour before he delivered it–yet, the deep understanding, the rugged spirit, the infinite compassion, the whole life of Lincoln thrills in its every word.

"Work–constantly, patiently, every day–striving toward the highest and the best. The moments of supreme action will come to you as they have come to all men we call great. The way of success is the way of struggle. Strive for perfection in the little things you do, and when the great moment comes you will be ready. You get your strength in the sweat of your body–in the tumult of your mind–in the aspiration of your soul.

"To win the race you must first be a slave at the galley's oar!"

And, before you start to run the race which is going to mean success or failure to you, there is a great lesson which you can learn from the little honey-bee–that of *persistency!*

It matters not how many times man robs the store-house of the bee, it will begin all over and replenish its supply of honey. No bee was ever known to wail or complain that someone had stolen the fruits of its labor. How unlike man the bee is in this respect. No bee ever quit trying as long as it was able to gather honey.

All down the road of life you will meet obstacles, many of them. Time after time failure will stare you in the face, but just remember this–that there is a great lesson in every obstacle you master and in every failure which you overcome. It is a part of Nature's plan to place obstacles in your way. Every time you master one of these you become stronger and better prepared for the next one. Obstacles are nothing more or less than necessary hurdles which train you and make you fit for the great race of life!

If you begin the New Year with a firm resolution to perform MORE work and BETTER work than you are paid to perform, you are apt to make this your most prosperous year.

Do not waste any time pitying the man who has met with many reverses and overcome numberless obstacles; he will be able to take care of himself; but, if you have sympathy that you wish to squander, give it to the man who was born with a silver spoon in his mouth and who has never known what it is to go hungry, and who has never found it necessary to permit any desire to go unsatisfied. He is the fellow who really needs your sympathy; the others will know how to take care of themselves because

They have served their apprenticeship at the galley's oar!

Any fool can QUIT the job when things go wrong, but the man who has the right sort of stuff in him MASTERS the obstacles that made him want to quit and when he has done this he no longer wants to quit.

BILLBOARD 7

SELF-CONTROL

A Personal Inventory of My Thirty-Six Years of Experience

In this editorial Mr. Hill enumerates what he believes to be the greatest lessons he has learned from early childhood up to the present.

I have often heard the expression "if I had my life to live over I would live it differently!"

Personally I could not truthfully say that I would change anything that has happened in my life, if I were living it over. Not that I have made no mistakes, for indeed it seems to me that I have made more mistakes than the average man makes, but out of these mistakes has comes an awakening which has brought me real happiness and abundant opportunity to help others find this much sought state of mind.

Every year I live I am more convinced that the waste of life lies in the love we have not given, the powers we have not used, the selfish prudence that will risk nothing, and which, shirking pain, misses happiness as well.

I am convinced, beyond room for doubt, that there is a great lesson in every failure, and, that so-called failure is absolutely necessary before worth-while success can be attained.

I am convinced that a part of Nature's plan is to throw obstacles in a man's pathway, and, that the greatest part of one's education comes, not from books or teachers, but from constantly striving to overcome these obstacles.

I believe that Nature lays down obstacles in a man's pathway, just as the trainer lays down rails and hurdles for a horse to jump over while being trained to "pace."

Today is my birthday!

I shall celebrate it by doing my best to set down, for the readers for the little brown-covered messenger, some of the lessons which my failures have taught me.

Let us begin with my favorite hobby, namely, my belief that the only real happiness anyone ever experiences comes from helping others to find happiness.

It may be a mere coincident that practically twenty-five of my thirty-six years were very unhappy years, and, that I began to find happiness the very day I commenced helping others find it, but I do not believe so. I believe this is more than a coincident—I believe that it is in strict accordance with a Law of the universe.

My experience has taught me that a man can no more sow a crop of grief and expect to reap a harvest of happiness than one could sow thistles and expect to reap a crop of wheat. Through many years of careful study and analysis I have learned conclusively that that which a man *gives* comes back to him increased many times, even down to the finest detail, whether a mere thought or an overt act.

From a material, economic standpoint, one of the greatest truths I have learned is that it pays handsomely to render more service and better service than one is paid to render, for just as surely as this is done it is but a question of time until one is paid for more than he actually does.

This one practice of throwing one's heart into every task, regardless of the remuneration, will go further toward the achievement of material, monetary success than any other one thing that I could mention.

But this is hardly of less importance than the habit of forgiving and forgetting the wrongs our fellowmen commit against us. The habit of "striking back" at those who anger us is a weakness which is bound to degrade and work to the detriment of all who practice it.

I am convinced that no lesson which my life's experience has taught me has been more costly than the one which I learned by eternally exacting my "pound of flesh" and feeling it my duty to resent every insult and every injustice.

I am thoroughly convinced that one of the greatest lessons a man can learn is that of *self-control*. One can never exercise any very great amount of influence over others until he first learns to exercise control over himself. It seems to be of particular significance when I stop and consider that most of the world's great leaders were men who were slow to anger, and, that the greatest of all the leaders down the ages, who gave us the greatest philosophy the world has ever known, as it is laid down in the Golden Rule, was a man of tolerance and *self-control*.

I never won anything without hard labor and the exercise of my best judgment and careful planning and working long in advance. I had to train myself painfully and laboriously, not merely as regards my body, but as regards my soul and spirit.

–THEODORE ROOSEVELT

I am convinced that it is a grievous mistake for any person to start out with the belief that upon his shoulders rests the burden of "reforming" the world, or, of changing the natural order of human conduct. I believe that Nature's own plans are working out quite rapidly enough without the interference of those who would presume to try to rush Nature or in any way divert her course. Such presumption leads only to argument, contention and ill feelings.

I have learned, to my own satisfaction at least, that a man who agitates and works up ill feeling between his fellowmen, for any cause whatsoever, serves no real constructive purpose in life. It pays to boost and construct instead of knocking and tearing down.

When I began the publication of this magazine I

commenced making use of this principle by devoting my time and editorial pages to that which is constructive and overlooking that which is destructive.

Nothing which I have ever undertaken in all of my thirty-six years has proved as successful or brought me as much real happiness as my work on this little magazine has done. Almost from the very day that the first edition went on the newsstands success has crowned my efforts in greater abundance than I had ever hoped for. Not necessarily monetary success, but that higher, finer success which is manifested in the happiness which this magazine has helped others to find.

I have found, from many years of experience, that it is a sign of weakness if a man permits himself to be influenced against one of his fellowmen on account of some remark made by an enemy or someone who is prejudiced. A man cannot truly claim to possess *self-control* or the ability to think clearly until he learns to form opinions of his fellowmen, not from someone else's viewpoint, but from actual knowledge.

One of the most detrimental and destructive habits which I have had to overcome has been that of allowing myself to be influenced against a person by someone who was biased or prejudiced.

Another great mistake which I have learned by having made the same mistake over and over again, it that it is a grievous mistake to slander one's fellowmen, either *with* or *without* cause. I cannot recall any personal development which I have gained from my mistakes that has given me as much real satisfaction as that which I have experienced from the knowledge that I had, to some extent, learned to hold my tongue unless I could say something kind of my fellowmen.

I only learned to curb this natural human tendency of "picking one's enemies to pieces" after I began to understand the Law of Retaliation, through the operation of which a man is sure to reap that which he sows, either by word of mouth, or by action. I am by no means master of this evil, but I have at least made a fair start toward conquering it.

My experience has taught me that most men are inherently honest, and, that those whom we usually call dishonest are victims of circumstances over which they haven't full control. It has been a source of great benefit to me in editing this magazine to know that it is a natural tendency of people to live up to the reputation which their fellowmen give them.

I am convinced that every man should go through that biting, through valuable experience of having been attacked by the newspapers and losing his fortune, at least once in his lifetime, because it is when calamity overtakes a man that he learns who his real friends are. The friends stay by the ship while the "would-be's" make for cover.

I have learned, among other interesting bits of knowledge of human nature that a man can by very accurately judged by the character of people whom he attracts to him. That old axiomatic phrase, "birds of a feather flock together", is sound philosophy.

Throughout the universe this Law of Attraction, as it might be called, continuously attracts to certain centers, things of a like nature. A great detective once told me that this Law of Attraction was his chief dependence in hunting down criminals and those charged with breaking the law.

I have learned that the man who aspires to be a public servant must be prepared to sacrifice much and withstand abuse and criticism without losing faith in or respect for his fellowmen. It is rare indeed to find a man engaged in serving the public whose motives are not questioned by the very people whom his efforts benefit most.

The greatest servant the world has ever known not only gained the ill-will of many of the people of his time–an ill-will to which a great many of the present age have fallen heir–but he lost his life in the bargain. They nailed him to a cross, pierced his side with a spear and fiendishly tortured him by spitting in his face while his life slowly ebbed away. He set us a mighty fine example to follow in his last words, which were something like the following: "Forgive them, Father, for they know not what they do."

When I feel my blood rushing to my head in anger on account of the wrongs which my fellowmen do me, I find comfort in the fortitude and the patience with which the great Philosopher watched his tormentors as they slowly put him to death, for no offense whatsoever except that of trying to help his fellowmen find happiness.

My experience has taught me that the man who accuses the world of not giving him a chance to succeed in his chosen work, instead of pointing the accusing finger at himself, seldom finds his name in Who's Who.

A "chance to succeed" is something which every man must go out and create for himself. Without a certain degree of combativeness a person is not apt to accomplish very much in this world, or acquire anything which other people covet very highly. Without combativeness a man can easily inherit poverty, misery and failure, but if he gets a grip on the opposite to these he must be prepared to "contend" for his *rights!*

But; note well that we said his "rights"!

The only "rights" a man has are those which he *creates* for himself in return for service rendered; and, it may not be a bad idea to remind ourselves that the nature of those "rights" will correspond exactly to the nature of the service rendered.

My experience has taught me that a child can be burdened with no heavier a load nor visited with a greater curse than that which accompanies the indiscriminate use of wealth. A close analysis of history will show that most of the great servants of the public and of humanity were people who arose from poverty.

In my opinion a real test of a man is to give him unlimited wealth and see what he will do with it. Wealth which takes away the incentive to engage in constructive, useful work, is a curse to those who so use it. It is not poverty that a man needs to watch–it is wealth and the attendant power which wealth creates, for good or for evil ends.

I consider it very fortunate that I was born in poverty, while in my more mature years I have associated rather closely with men of wealth, thus I have had a very fair demonstration of the effect of these two widely separated positions. I know I shall not need to watch myself so very closely as long as the need for life's ordinary necessities confronts me, but if I should gain great wealth it would be quite essential for me to see that this did not take away the desire to serve my fellowmen.

My experience has taught me that a normal person can accomplish anything possible of human accomplishment, through the aid of the human mind. The greatest thing which the human mind can do is to *imagine!* The so-called genius is merely a person who has created something definite in his mind, through imagination, and then transformed that picture into reality, through bodily action.

A man is relieved and gay when he has put his heart into his work and done his best; but what he has said and done otherwise shall give him no peace.

–EMERSON

All this, and a little more, have I learned during these past thirty-six years, but the greatest thing I have learned is that old, old truth of which the philosophers all down the ages have told us, that *happiness* is found, not in possession, but in useful service!

This is a truth which one can appreciate only after having discovered it for himself!

There may be many ways through which I could find greater happiness than that which I receive in return for the work which I devote to the editing of this little magazine, but frankly I have not discovered it, nor do I expect to.

The only thing I can think of which would bring me a greater measure of happiness than I already have would be a larger number of people to serve through the little brown-covered messenger of good-cheer and enthusiasm.

I believe the happiest moment of my life was experienced a

few weeks ago, while I was making a small purchase in a store in Dallas, Texas. The young man who was waiting on me was a rather sociable, talkative, thinking type of young fellow. He told me all about what was going on in the store–a sort of "behind the curtains" visit, as it were–and wound up by telling me that his store manager had made all of his people very happy that day be promising them a Golden Rule Psychology Club and a subscription to Hill's Golden Rule Magazine, with the store's compliments.

(No, he didn't know who I was.)

That interested me, naturally, so I asked him who this Napoleon Hill was, about whom he had been talking. He looked at me with a quizzical expression on his face and replied: "You mean to say you never heard of Napoleon Hill"? I confessed that the name did sound rather familiar, but I asked the young man what it was that caused his store manger to give each of his employees a year's subscription to Hill's Golden Rule, and he said: "Because one month's issue of it has converted one of the grouchiest men we've got, into one of the best fellows in this store, and my boss said if it would do that he wanted all of us to read it."

It was not the appeal to my egotistical side which made me happy as I shook hands with the young man and told him who I was, but to that deeper emotional side which is always touched in every human being when he finds that his work is bringing happiness to others.

This is the sort of happiness which modifies the common human tendency toward selfishness, and aids evolution in its work of separating the animal instincts from the human intuition in human beings.

I have always contended that a man should develop self-confidence, and, that he should be a good self-advertisement, and I am going to prove that I practice that which I preach on this subject by boldly asserting that if I had an audience as great as that which is served by The Saturday Evening Post, which I could serve monthly through this little magazine, I could accomplish more inside of the next five years toward influencing the masses to deal with each other on the Golden Rule basis, than all the other newspapers and magazines combined have done in the last ten years.

The enormous new found power, industrial and political, which the workers have acquired, can be wasted by a reckless use of it in needless stoppages and strikes. If labor is ever to think of itself as a controlling force in the nation it must cease to think of itself in the terms of class as it has hitherto.

–CLYNES, ENGLISH LABOR LEADER

This, the December issue of the Golden Rule, marks the end of our first year, and I know it will not be construed as an idle boast when I tell my readers that the seed which we have sown through these pages during these twelve months are beginning to sprout and grow throughout the United States, Canada and some of the other foreign countries, and, that some of the greatest philosophers, teachers, preachers and business men of the age have not only pledged us their hearty moral support, but they have actually gone out and rounded up subscriptions for us in order to help foster the spirit of good-will which we are preaching.

Is it any wonder that your humble editor is happy?

There are men who have more, much more, of the worldly wealth to show for their thirty-six years of experience than the writer has, but I have no fear in challenging all of them to show a greater stock of happiness than I enjoy as a result of my work.

Of course it may be only a meaningless circumstance, but to me it is quite significant that the greatest and deepest happiness which I have experienced has come to me ever since I began publishing this magazine.

"Whatsoever a man soweth that shall he also reap."

Yes, it came from the Bible, and it is sound philosophy which always works. And my thirty years of experience has proved conclusively that I does.

The first time the notion ever struck me to own and edit a magazine, some fifteen years ago, my idea was to jump on everything that was bad and pick to pieces all that I did not like. The gods of fate must have intervened to keep me from starting such an enterprise at that time, because everything that I have learned in my thirty-six years of experience fully corroborates the philosophy in the above quotation.

You can never become a great leader nor a person of influence in the cause of justice until you have developed great *self-control*.

Before you can be of great service to your fellow men in any capacity you must master the common human tendency of anger, intolerance and cynicism.

When you permit another person to make you angry you are allowing that person to dominate you and drag you down to his level.

To develop *self-control* you must make liberal and systematic use of the Golden Rule philosophy; you must acquire the habit of forgiving those who annoy and arouse you to anger.

Intolerance and selfishness make very poor bed-fellows for self-control. These qualities always clash when you try to house them together. One or the other must get out.

The first thing the shrewd lawyer usually does when he starts to cross-examine a witness is to make the witness angry and thereby cause him to lose his self-control.

Anger is a state of insanity!

The well-balanced person is a person who is slow to anger and who always remains cool and calculating in his procedure. He remains calm and deliberate under all conditions.

Such a person can succeed in all legitimate undertaking! To master conditions you must first master self! A person who exercises great *self-control* never slanders his neighbor. His tendency is to build up and not to tear down. Are you a person of *self-control*. If not, why do you not develop this great virtue?

BILLBOARD 8

HABIT OF PERFORMING MORE WORK THAN PAID FOR

From Poverty to Wealth Through Struggle

The eighth billboard on the road to success is the *habit of performing more work than paid for.*

The Story of Edwin C. Barnes who rode into East Orange, New Jersey, on a freight car, less than fifteen years ago, secured a job from Thomas A. Edison, and is now retiring with all the money he needs, at the age of forty.

This is another story of success that grew out of struggle, plus the application of those fundamentals of which we are writing in the pages of this magazine every month. The editor of this magazine knows Edwin C. Barnes, intimately, and is qualified, therefore, to write authentically concerning those qualities through which Mr. Barnes has mastered poverty and risen to a high position of respect among men, in a comparatively short period of time.

–EDITOR

Ten years ago I walked into Edwin C. Barnes office, in the city of Chicago, to ask a simple question concerning a subject in which Mr. Barnes was in no way interested.

It so happened that I met Mr. Barnes, personally, as he was passing through the waiting room of his offices.

If I should live to be a hundred and fifty I will never forget the manner in which he stopped and went into full details in answer to my questions.

I wanted to know if Mr. Edison's factory would manufacture a series of phonograph records for me, which I had in mind using in teaching course in Public Speaking.

No, Mr. Barnes did not believe Mr. Edison's plant was making special records, but, perhaps he could direct me to someone who would accommodate me, so he put on his hat, took me in his automobile and carried me to see a competitor many miles away, in another part of the city.

There was not the slightest chance of this act resulting in a business advantage to Mr. Barnes, and he well knew it, therefore it is reasonable to assume that he rendered me this service only because it was his nature to render service wherever and to whomsoever possible, regardless of immediate or ultimate returns to him personally.

Naturally Mr. Barnes' courtesy made a "hit" with me. I commenced to study him because I believed him to be worth emulating. I noticed that an atmosphere of cordiality and enthusiasm permeated his offices. I saw that every one of his salesmen and his stenographers and his information girl and all the rest looked as if they were glad to be there.

That was ten years ago. I venture the suggestion that if you went into one of Mr. Barnes' offices today, in the cities of Chicago, St. Louis or New York, unannounced, and asked for some favor you would get the same impression which I got ten years ago; namely, that you were in an office where courtesy was extended because those extending it believed in it.

Mr. Barnes won his way into Thomas A. Edison's confidence and got Mr. Edison to give him a job. If I remember correctly the salary was less than $25.00 a week. Shortly afterward he won his way further into Mr. Edison's confidence and got the agency for the "Ediphone" (Edison Dictating Machine) for the city of Chicago. I do not know the exact modus operandi through which he sold Mr. Edison, but with this I am sure all who know Mr. Edison will heartily agree–that he did not win it except by producing results and rendering more service and *better service than he was actually paid to render*. I am sure he did not quibble about either hours or pay, in the beginning, and I am sure he put in much more time than he agreed to put in.

From the very beginning Mr. Barnes adopted the policy of never selling an "Ediphone" dictating machine where it was not needed, or a single machine more than was necessary to handle the purchaser's business efficiently. Sometimes his salesmen, in their eagerness to pile up records would talk a customer into over-buying. Invariably Mr. Barnes would scrutinize such transactions, detect the mistake and give the salesman a chance to undo it before it undid the salesman and also the firm for which he worked.

A man of striking personality, friendly, congenial and enthusiastic, Mr. Barnes was naturally an able salesman, but he never could have succeeded as he has done except through the application of rendering more service and better service than he contracted to deliver. With him this principle seemed to come naturally. It was a part of him.

Mr. Barnes' business was no easy one to establish. Dictating machines were a novelty twelve or fifteen years ago, and it required the highest order of salesmanship to sell them, and a still higher order of salesmanship to get people to learn to use them after they were sold. In truth these machines save practically half of the stenographer's time, but, like every other new invention on earth, from the steamboat to the flying machine, people "had to be shown."

Edwin C. Barnes sells practically the entire output of "Ediphones" produced in the great factories of Thomas A. Edison, at East Orange, New Jersey. When I think of him I cannot help reflecting upon my visit with seven down-and-outers whom I interviewed in Chicago a few years ago, one of them a graduate of Yale University.

Everyone of these chaps complained that the "world would not give me a chance."

I thought of Edwin Barnes while I was conducting these interviews, and I wondered if the world gave him any better chance than it gave those seven men whom I was interviewing, and who charged the world with the cause of his failure.

His entre into East Orange was not very pretentious. He went there on "blind baggage," found Mr. Edison, made him listen, and got a chance to prove to Mr. Edison that he did not believe the world owed him a living.

Mr. Barnes' story is exactly the same as that of every other man who was succeeded. He has rendered service first and collected afterward. Instead of waiting for the world to come around and pay up the living it owes him, he has gone out and rendered the world a service that has brought him a fortune, and this while he is yet a comparatively young man.

I do not know how much Mr. Barnes is worth, but it is considerable. He lives in Florida, where he takes life easy most of the year. The remainder of the time is spent in visiting his business associates who are still conducting his business of marketing the "Ediphone" in the cities of Chicago, St. Louis and New York.

An interesting thing happened just a few days ago, that will throw a side-light on the Barnes way of doing things. I came to our New York office, from Chicago, but on my way I stopped in to see Mr. Barnes at his office on lower Broadway. I had my hand-bag with me. I left it at his office while I went out to look up a permanent place to live, as I had come to New York to stay. As I started to leave he called me back and said: "We close the office at six o'clock. If you are not back by that time I will carry your bag over to your hotel for you, if you will telephone me where you stop."

And, he meant what he said. Think of it–a man of his wealth and position and success, offering to lug my hand-bag around from me! It supports the theory that he who would be great amongst us must first be the best servant. Service, rendered in the right spirit, cannot fail to elevate the person who renders it. The Master said so, two thousand years ago, and every successful man could say so. Barnes has succeeded because he has *served* well. He has not been afraid to ride the bumpers or do anything else that had to be done in order to carry his "Message to Garcia."

We struggle for fame, and win it; and, lo! Like a fleeting breath, it is lost in the realm of silence, whose ruler and king is Death.

At a meeting of the Thomas A. Edison organization recently, at which Mr. Barnes and more than one hundred of the Edison representatives were present, an incident happened that throws an interesting sidelight on both Barnes and Edison.

The "wizard" had just been presented with a commemorative silk flag. The presentation speech was made by George M. Austin, of Philadelphia. Mr. Edison was to reply, but instead his speech was read by his son, Charles Edison. While the son was reading the speech, Mr. Edison took off his right shoe, got a jack knife and cut a piece of leather, which was hanging from the sole.

The gathering watching the inventor paused and then broke out in a hearty burst of laughter.

The inventor joined in the laugh and said:

Beating the Profiteer

"I went over to New York to buy a pair of shoes and found they were asking $17 and $18 a pair. I went down to Cortlandt Street and in a cellar I noticed a lot of shoes. I saw a pair that struck my fancy and bought them for $6. I have been wearing that pair of shoes for nearly a year."

Standing near Mr. Edison was Edwin C. Barnes, head of the New York, Chicago and St. Louis division.

Edison pointed to Barnes and said:

"Barnes would not have done it that way. He would have gone up on Broadway and paid $17 or $18 a pair."

"Yes, but I would wear them for three or four years," said Barnes.

"Ed Barnes pays $6 or $7 for a hat," said Mr. Edison, "while I would go over to New York or down to Newark and pay $2.75 for one."

Edison then produced several yellow slips, and said that every night he made a list of what he intended to do. Today's list contained fifty-seven different matters that he expected to attend to.

"If everybody tried it for six months it would be a surprise to see how much could be accomplished in ten hours," said Mr. Edison.

With all of his wealth and all of his success and his scores of friends, ranging all the way from such men as ex-President Theodore Roosevelt, on down to Napoleon Hill, Mr. Barnes remains democratic and approachable by anyone who wants to see him. Not so much as a private secretary stands between his office door and the reception room. His secretary is busy looking after more important business than that of heading off people who want to see Mr. Barnes. His theory is that if anyone comes to his office to see him that person is honoring him by so doing, therefore he will be just as good a sportsman and give that person a hearing, no matter what may be wanted.

Every time I think of Barnes I think of the United States Senate. He is just the type of a man we need down at Washington. He believes in serving rather than being served, and if the people of Florida were fortunate enough to get him to accept a Senatorship they would have room to congratulate themselves, because he would be a servant indeed while he was in Washington.

I believe the Senate could well afford a few more real servants, with such business ability as Mr. Barnes has, and whose integrity is irreproachable. It seems to me that it would in no way be inimical to the interests of the people if we had a few more successful business men in the Senate and a few less professional politicians who go there for the sole purpose of trading in political favors.

Barnes would be such a man. He has the ability. He has the personality to make his presence felt among any body of men. He has the courage to fight where fighting is necessary and the diplomacy to trade where trading is better than a fight.

Citizens of Florida, we commend to you your citizen, Edwin C. Barnes, of Bradentown, Florida, and suggest that you will be fortunate indeed if you can get him to consent to serve you as United States Senator, because he will serve you as well and as successfully as he has served Thomas A. Edison.

If this writer is not mistaken there is only one just basis upon which to sell personal service and that is the basis of compensation which is proportionate to the *quality* and the *quantity* of service rendered.

One man is working at a lathe, receiving, let us say $5.00 a day for his services. He has been in that job for several years. Another man comes along and takes the lathe next to him. He has been in that job but a few days. He is doing exactly the same class of work, but he does one-fourth more than the man who has been there for several years.

Which should receive the highest wages?

The answer is obvious! The length of time an employee has been on a job has nothing whatsoever to do with the wages he should receive. If it did the old janitor who takes care of the building in which I have my offices would be receiving more wages than the superintendent of the building, because he has been here for ten years while the superintendent has held his job less than six months.

There is one important thing for you to remember in marketing your personal services, and it is this: *Your efficiency in your work and your value to your employer can be very accurately determined by the amount of supervision which you require.* If you require but little supervision you are apt to be fairly efficient. If you require no supervision at all you probably have reached the height of efficiency in the work you are doing, therefore the next move is to assume work which carries greater responsibilities.

You might as well understand that you are not apt to receive very much for your services until you are prepared to assume heavy responsibilities. The big salaries are paid to men who can efficiently and satisfactorily shoulder responsibilities and assume the leadership of others.

It is impossible for any man to earn $25,000 a year with his hands alone, but he may be worth four times that amount if he can assume the leadership of thousands of others and help them add something to their efficiency and their ability to use their hands.

The two chief qualities which have taken so many thousands of men from the rank and file of ordinary labor and placed them in responsible executive positions are:

First: The ability plus the willingness to assume heavy responsibilities.

Second: The ability to help other men and women perform more efficient work, by intelligently guiding them in their efforts.

It is not a mere idealistic axiom–*we get that which we give!* It is a sound fundamental truth upon which all successful men work. The man who *gets* the most from the sale of his personal services is the man who *gives* the most to those for whom he works, whether his job is to manage himself with but little or no supervision, or to help others intelligently direct their efforts.

It is not the man who can dispose of the most details with his own hands who is sought for the job higher up–it is the man who has the ability, plus the good judgment, to get others to take care of details. If you are aiming for one of the "higher-up" jobs, may it not be well for you to begin now to teach others how to handle the details of your present job?

If you have been in the same position for a long while and your pay remains the same, it is more than likely that you have not sought the opportunity to take on greater responsibilities, and it is also quite likely that you require as much supervision now as you did in the past. These two qualities act as a guide post if you will observe them. You can measure yourself by them very accurately.

You will not be prepared to assume greater responsibilities or the leadership and direction of other workers until you have brought your own efficiency up to the high water mark. The chances are that you cannot get others to do more work or better work than you, yourself, make a practice of doing!

Leadership develops out of the good example you set for others to follow. When you begin to lead your fellow workers in *quality* and *quantity* of work you will be on the road to a bigger job, at better pay and with greater responsibilities.

Difficulties are never settled while passion rages. They are never permanently settled by conflict. One party may be subdued by power, but the sense of wrong will remain; the fire of passion will slumber, ready to break out again on the first occasion. Let us take Golden Rule as a guide and all cause for hostility will be removed, all conflict will cease, and humanity will go hand in hand to do its work and reap it's just reward.

We do not recall ever having heard of any man being placed in a big executive job all at one jump, but we could name hundreds of executives who got into their positions slowly, step by step, by gradually increasing their own efficiency and improving the *quality* and *quantity* of their work.

When I urge upon you the necessity of *doing more work and better work than you are actually paid to do* I do so, not for idealistic reasons, but because I know that this principle is good business on your part. It is sound economy. It is sound because it will *automatically attract to you the good will and cooperation of all with whom you work, including your employer.* If it does not get the attention of your present employer (as it probably will) then it will attract to you some other employer who will seek you out and offer you a bigger and better job.

If I am not mistaken the best way on earth to market

personal services to the greatest advantage is by attracting an employer on account of work that is better than that of the average worker. When an employer seeks you out you may rest assured that you will be able to command a higher salary than you would if you sought the employer, and the only way to cause an employer to seek you is by performing services which are above the average in quantity and quality.

This applies to the man who is in a small job and wants a bigger one with the same employer, just the same as it does to the man who wishes to change employers.

I envy the man who has the sound judgment to enable him to see that it pays to perform more work and better work than he is paid to perform, and to assume responsibilities to his full capacity instead of pushing them off onto George. I envy him, because he is one in ten thousand. That is why he is at the head instead of the foot in his calling. That is why he is drawing a salary instead of "wages." That is why he is placed in charge of others.

In the office next to mine is a young man who holds the job of business manager of this magazine. When he came to get the job he asked no such foolish questions as "What does this job pay?" "What will the hours be?" "Has it any possibilities?" "When will I get a raise?" "Will there be any night work in it?"

No, he asked no such questions as these!

He took me off my feet by telling me how much he really knew about the magazine, notwithstanding the fact that the first issue of it had been on the newsstands only one day. He said he had come to go to work on the Golden Rule and that he intended to get what he came after unless I threw him out of the office. He convinced me that he wanted that job because he believed in the work back of it.

He did not ask how soon I would give him an assistant, but instead he asked *"What shall I do first?"*

His name is W. H. Heggem!

Remember the name if you want to, but I can tell you fellows who are constantly on the lookout for live wires that I do not want you "snooping" around the Golden Rule offices trying to get him away from me. Oh, you'll want him, but wait a minute–*his earnings this year probably will go well beyond the $10,000 a year mark!*

Yes, he is worth it, and I shall be as glad to pay it to him as he will be to receive it. I am just like all other men who employ people–*I want the best service to be had and I am willing to pay for all that any of my associate workers can deliver.* I might be willing to pay more than they actually produce, but for economic reasons I could not keep this up indefinitely. No man can pay out money in wages and salaries which he is not producing out of the business and keep it up indefinitely. The spring soon runs dry unless it is constantly replenished.

If you feel that your employer should pay you more money than you are getting there is only one just basis upon which to ask for that extra money and that is by first changing the nature of your work and making it produce greater returns for your employer.

Perhaps you are a bookkeeper, let us say, and you do not see how you can render service that is greater in quantity or better in quality. You are working long hours as it is, and you are doing the best work that you know how to perform.

What can you do that will entitle you to more than you receive?

There are a dozen lines of procedure, any of which would answer this question, but to try to follow a dozen different routes is equivalent of following no route. What you really want is exactly *one* line of procedure.

You are the bookkeeper. You make up the monthly statements of accounts and mail them out. May it not be possible that you can create a collection system which will turn those accounts into ready cash as fast as they become due? If you can do this is it not probable that your employer will be glad to pay you in proportion to the results you get?

You can broaden the scope of your responsibilities by voluntarily performing more work than that of merely keeping the books. You can do this without in any way decreasing your efficiency in your bookkeeping work. Work out a series of collection letters which will create good-will for your employer and at the same time collect the money that is due him.

Most any old top can do it when someone tells him to and shows him how, but what the man who furnishes the payroll wants is a man who sees what ought to be done and goes ahead and does it without being told.

The law of supply and demand sets a certain general average salary that an ordinary bookkeeper can command. To get more than this he must perform some service which is not usually performed by the "ordinary" bookkeeper. In brief, he must take himself out of the "ordinary" class or else be satisfied with "ordinary" wages.

There is nothing sentimental about this practice of performing *more work and better work than one is paid to perform.* It is simply sound business practice. Of course, if you perform your work in a cheerful, enthusiastic spirit you will likely attract people to you more readily.

You will be much more apt to succeed in a big way if you develop an attractive, pleasing personality along with the *habit of performing more work and better work than you are paid to perform.* In fact, a pleasing personality may be laid down as a necessary qualification for success in any undertaking in which one is serving others.

BILLBOARD 9

ATTRACTIVE PERSONALITY

The ninth billboard on the road to success is *attractive personality.*

My heart goes out to the man who walks the streets looking for a job. It is the most discouraging task a human being ever performed. I earnestly wish I might reach every man and woman on earth who are out of employment and give them the pass key to whatever position they are prepared to fill.

I will tell you what this key is in very words in which I passed it on to a reader of the Golden Rule who came to see me today. He was out of a job. He had called on more than a dozen firms but they had all turned him down.

I asked him to tell me exactly what he had said when he asked for employment. He described his canvass by saying that he had simply gone in and asked if there was a position open. Before receiving a reply he had stated that he was out of employment and would be willing to accept any reasonable salary as a starter.

He was turned away as rapidly as he applied.

The reason was obvious. Why I think so is disclosed by what I said to him. First, I asked him to stand up so I could look him over just as the person to whom he applied for work had done. He had on a pair of shoes that were run down at the heels. He wore a cap. Otherwise his clothes were becoming.

These were my suggestions to him: Go out and have a shoemaker build up your heels. This will give you a feeling of greater self-confidence, something that you will need. Buy yourself a hat that is becoming and throw away that cap. This will make you feel like a man instead of a boy and give you a dignified look that you will need.

Decide exactly what position you wish to get and the firm that you wish to work for. Go out and find out all you can about the firm and be prepared to give some good reasons why you believe you can serve it in the position you seek.

Then go to the firm and say this:

"I have decided to accept a position with you. You don't know it, but that's what I am here for. I want such and such a position which I know I can fill in a manner that will be profitable to you. I am ready to go to work right now if you will tell me where I will find a peg to hang my hat and coat on. *Oh yes, the salary! Suppose we forget about that until you have seen me in the harness for a week. Then if you feel that I have earned anything you may put it in my pay envelope."*

He followed my suggestions. In less than two hours he was back at my office. His heels had been built up. His hair had been trimmed. He had exchanged the frown on his face for a smile. I pronounced him ready for the trial. He left and in less than an hour telephoned me that he was at work in the new job.

There are different ideas as to what success is, but whether your idea of success is the accumulation of wealth or the rendering of some great service to mankind, or both, you will not likely achieve it unless you have a definite plan of procedure mapped out.

In the last ten years I suppose I have passed this idea on to more than a hundred people, and in every single case, as far as I have any knowledge of the results, it has worked successfully.

I tell you the business world is looking for the man who has enough confidence in himself to go to work on these terms. In ninety-nine cases out of a hundred a man will parley, argue and do everything possible to persuade a prospective employer to start him at the highest possible salary.

There is only one true basis for the payment of money in return for personal services and it is this: a man is entitled to remuneration in proportion to the quality and quantity of service he renders. The experience he has had, his age, his ability and his standing have nothing to do with the salary he should receive. Nothing but the *service he renders* counts.

You need have no fear of competition from the man who says, "I'm not paid to do that, therefore I'll not do it." He will never be a dangerous competitor for your job; but watch out for the fellow who stays at his desk or work bench until his work is finished–watch out that such fellow does not "challenge you at the post and pass you at the grandstand."

In prosperous times like these there is absolutely no reason for any person walking the streets without employment. Through the use of this plan, whether by personal application or by letter, any man who needs the kind of services that you can render is more than apt to give you a trial.

And a trial is all you want. If you don't make good you'll be slated for the exit skids anyway, whether you go to work under this plan or at an agreed salary.

Many a capable man has been floored when applying for a position, by this question: "*What experience have you had?*" Now he may not have had very much experience, but deep down in his heart he knows he can do the work and do it well. Honor demands that he reply truthfully which usually means that the interview ends right there.

Now if you are ever confronted with this sort of a situation suppose you say: "Now look here–don't you believe that a sample of my work would answer your question better than anything *I might say about myself?* Naturally I am prejudiced in my own behalf, but if you'll show me a place to hang my hat and coat I'll jump in and show you what I can do, on my own time, and if you don't like my work you shall not pay me a cent for it."

That ends the matter. Most men will give you the chance

you ask for.

If you have doubts that this plan will work you can try it out and convince yourself that it will. Write a dozen letters to as many different firms. I will tell you how to word the first paragraph and it will not make much difference how you word the remainder of the letter. Write it as follows:

"I have made up my mind to go to work for you and one of the qualities with which I am blessed is the bull-dog persistency of coming back with whatever I go after. I want the position of..................and my salary to begin with is to be zero and to remain at that figure until I have made myself so valuable to you that you will want to keep me and pay me in proportion to the *quality* and *quantity of work I perform."*

The foregoing is the sum and substance that should mark the opening of your letter. It will bring results. Out of twelve letters you ought to receive six acceptances if you use care in the selection of those to whom you send these letters.

In the closing paragraphs of your letter you will, of course, give full information concerning yourself and state just why you believe you can fill the position you seek, give references and the like. This will save time and eliminate useless correspondence.

Twelve years ago a freight train rolled into East Orange, New Jersey, carrying a passenger who rode without a pass or ticket. He went to that New Jersey city for a specific purpose and that was to get a job with Thomas A. Edison.

He got what he went after! His name is Edwin C. Barnes.

His wages to start with were $25.00 a week but they did not remain at that figure long. The old man Edison himself saw that Barnes had one quality which made him desirable, not merely as a department manager, but as a partner in a branch of the great Edison industries.

That quality is the same one which this writer mentioned in the editorial on the first page of the January edition of this magazine, namely–the habit of performing more work than one is paid to perform.

Edwin C. Barnes is your editor's close personal friend, a friend whom he greatly admires, but this is not the reason why Mr. Barnes is mentioned in these columns. He is mentioned because he is a living example of the soundness of the policy of performing more work than is paid for.

When Mr. Barnes presented himself to Edison, just after alighting from the "blind baggage" that brought him to town, there was no job open for him. Something that he said to Mr. Edison during the interview nearly cost him his chance to become a partner of the world's greatest scientist and inventor, but it turned out to be the influence that got him his "trial." During the conversation he said to Mr. Edison:

"You know I don't have to work"—and just as Mr. Edison was opening the door to show him the way out Barnes finished the sentence—"I could starve to death." This tickled Edison who saw that a man who could joke like that on an empty stomach might become a pretty fair worker on a full stomach, so he hired him without further questioning.

I do not know what Mr. Barnes' personal income is, but I do know that his interest in the Edison enterprise is easily worth $100,000.00 if not more. This represents the returns for his services covering a period of twelve years. It is not as well as some men have done, but it is much better than a great many others have done.

Mr. Barnes employs scores of salesmen who sell the "Ediphone." He has a notion that no salesman ought to sell a machine unless it is needed by the purchaser. Furthermore, he makes it his business to see that no salesman sells any firm or individual more machines than can be used economically.

When an "Ediphone" is installed does Barnes divide the profit on the machine with the old man Edison and then promptly forget about the transaction?

On your life he does not!

His idea is that dictating machine has not been sold until it has served the buyer satisfactorily during its natural life, which is a great many years. Every month Barnes sends a man around to look over every "Ediphone" in use, and to see that it is serving the purchaser satisfactorily.

There are other dictating machines on the market–probably as good as the "Ediphone"–but as far as the writer has ever been able to ascertain there is only one "Barnes-Edison Service" sold with a dictating machine.

As a partner in the Edison dictating machine industry Mr. Barnes covers just three cities–Chicago, New York and St. Louis. There are at least a dozen other cities in the United States waiting for a counterpart of Edwin C. Barnes to come along and develop them as a partner of Thomas A. Edison, just as Barnes has done in these three cities.

Freight trains continue to run into East Orange. Mr. Edison is still in business there. If you really and truly believe in the practice of performing more work than you are paid to perform and are willing to begin in the way that Barnes began you can become an Edison partner.

It may be that you do not care to enter the business that Mr. Barnes is engaged in. Probably a partnership with Charles M. Schwab, in the steel business, would suit you better. Or, a partnership with Rockefeller, in the oil business, or with Morgan in the banking business. You can get into any of these great enterprises if you make up your mind to do so.

The chances are that your present job has just as great possibilities as any of these would have. You can duplicate Edwin C. Barnes' success without going to work for Edison. Selling dictating machines is about the hardest sort of selling. It is hard because you have to convince the stenographer that the machine will enable her to perform at least twice as much work in a day as she could perform without it, and that her salary probably will eventually be regulated accordingly. Then you have to convince the man who pays for the machine that it not only costs him nothing in the run of a year's business use, but that it actually saves him many times its original cost.

Neither of these tasks is easy of accomplishment, therefore you may find it more desirable to stay right where you are. If your employer happens not to be as successful as Edison perhaps this condition offers you your big opportunity. Nobody told Barnes how to induce Edison to take him into partnership, and no one can tell you how to induce your employer to do it, but if you make up your mind to get there you will, just as Barnes did. You'll find the way.

I know Edwin C. Barnes intimately. He has no more brains or ability than many another who is not doing half as well. The secret of his success is not superior brains, not "pull," not "luck," but the habit of doing all the useful work he can without regard to the money that he receives for it.

The first time this writer ever saw Mr. Barnes we met by mere accident. I went into his office to ask for some information and happened to meet him coming out of his office. He not only gave me the information I sought, but he took me in his automobile to see a man who knew more about the subject on which I sought information than Mr. Barnes did. He went a long way out of his path to accommodate a man whom he had never seen before and whom he probably never expected to see again.

But that was the Barnes way! It was the way which attracted Edison to him. It was the way which has attracted many a big purchaser of the "Ediphone" to him, even in the face of strong competition by other salesmen of dictating machines.

When a man buys an "Ediphone" from Barnes he knows that he is getting more than a mere mechanical contrivance which takes dictation accurately, at any rate of speed and at all hours of the day—he knows that he is getting a service which greatly enhances the value of that machine. Whether you are selling your services in a grocery store, a coal mine or some other place, you can deliver that service in such a way that the purchaser will feel that he is getting something from you that he wouldn't get from any other person.

That "feeling" is one of the chief reasons why men will seek you out as a future foreman, department manager, superintendent or partner in their business.

You want to succeed!

We all do. What, then, is success? In the estimation of this writer success is the achievement of one's Chief Aim in life. It may be the getting of money or it may be the acquiring of leadership some great cause that will benefit humanity.

A crowd of troubles passed me by
As I with courage waited;
Said I, "Where do your troubles fly
When you are thus belated?"
"We go," they said, "to those who mope,
Who look on life dejected,
Who weakly say goodbye to hope–
We go where we're expected."

BILLBOARD 10

ACCURATE THOUGHT

The tenth billboard on the road to success is *accurate thought.*

To achieve fame or accumulate a big fortune requires the co-operation of your fellowmen. Whatever position one holds and whatever fortune one acquires must, to be permanent, be by sufferance of one's fellowmen.

You could no more remain in a position of honor without the good will of the neighborhood than you could fly to the moon, and as for holding a big fortune without the consent of your fellowmen it would be impossible, not only to hold it, but to acquire it in the first place, except by inheritance.

The peaceful enjoyment of money or position surely depends upon the extent to which you attract people to you. It does not require the farsighted philosopher to see that a man who enjoys the good will of all with whom he comes in contact can have anything within the gift of the people with whom he associates.

The roadway, then, to fame and fortune, or either, leads straight through the hearts of one's fellowmen.

There may be other ways of gaining the good will of one's fellowmen except through the operation of the Law of Retaliation, but if there is this writer has never discovered it.

Through the Law of Retaliation you can induce people to send back to you that which you give to them. There is no guess work about this–no element of chance–no uncertainty.

Let us see just how to go about harnessing this Law so it will work for us instead of against us. To begin with we need not tell you that the tendency of the human heart is to strike back, returning, stroke for stroke, every effort, whether of co-operation or of antagonism.

Antagonize a person and, as surely as two and two are four that person will retaliate in kind. Befriend a person or confer upon him some act of kindness and he will also reciprocate in kind.

Never mind the person who does not respond in accordance with this principle. He is merely the proverbial exception. By the law of averages the great majority of people will quite unconsciously respond.

The man who goes about with a chip on his shoulder finds a dozen people a day who take delight in knocking it off, a fact to which you can easily subscribe if you have ever tried going about with a chip on your shoulder. You need no proof that the man who carries a smile on his face and who always has a word of kindness for everyone he meets is universally liked, while the opposite type is just as generally disliked.

Your thoughts are servants of your will. You are master in your own house, and you can entertain whatever guests you please. Man moulds himself by his thoughts as a sculptor moulds clay. Think success and you'll be successful–if you only think it hard enough and steady enough and long enough.

This Law of Retaliation is a powerful force which touches the whole universe, constantly attracting and repelling. You will find it in the heart of the acorn which falls to the ground, and, in response to the warmth of the sunlight, bursts forth into a tiny sprig consisting of two small leaves which finally grow and attracts to itself the necessary elements to constitute a sturdy oak tree.

No one ever heard of an acorn attracting to it anything except the cells out of which an oak tree grows. No one ever saw a tree which was half oak and half poplar. The center of the acorn forms affinities only with those elements which constitute an oak tree.

Every thought which finds abode in the human brain attracts elements after its kind, whether of destruction or construction, kindness or unkindness. You can no more concentrate your mind on hatred and dislike and expect a crop of the opposite brand than you could expect an acorn to develop into a poplar tree. It simply is not in harmony with the Law of Retaliation.

No matter if the world laugh at you, take your own self seriously. The mob laughs at what it does not understand, ridicules what it cannot comprehend. Too many men who have the fire of genius within never let it kindle into flame because they fear the laughter of the crowd. Forget what others think. The thing that matters is what you think of yourself, and that you believe in yourself.

Throughout the universe everything in the form of matter gravitates to certain centers of attraction. People of similar intellect and tendencies are attracted to each other. The human mind forms affinities only with other minds which are harmonious and have similar tendencies, therefore the class of person which you attract to you will depend upon the tendencies of your own mind. You control those tendencies and can direct them along any line you choose, attracting to you any sort of person you wish.

This is a law of Nature. It is an immutable law and it works whether we make conscious use of it or not.

The person who poisons the mind with unclean thoughts commits a greater sin than does he who poisons the drinking water, because a poisoned mind reproduces itself in other minds.

A Brief Story of the Human Mind

At birth the mind is a blank; a great storage room with nothing in it but space.

Through the five senses of seeing, hearing, tasting, smelling and feeling, this great storehouse is filled.

The sense impressions which find their way into this storehouse before the age of twelve, are apt to remain there throughout life, whether they are sound or unsound.

Ideals and beliefs which are planted in the young, plastic mind of a child, are apt to become a part of that child and remain with it throughout life.

It is possible to so impressively inject an ideal into a child's mind that this ideal will guide the child in its ethical conduct throughout life. It is possible to so thoroughly build character in the child's mind, before the age of twelve or fourteen years, that it would be practically impossible for that child to disregard that character and go wrong in after life.

The mind resembles a great, fertile field in that it will produce a crop after the kind of seed sown in it, by which is meant that any idea placed in the mind and held there firmly, will finally take root and grow, influencing the bodily action of the person after the nature of the idea. Also, just as wild weeds will spring up in fertile soil that is not tilled, so will destructive ideas find their way into the minds of those who have not planted there constructive ideas.

The mind cannot remain idle. It is always striving to produce, and, naturally enough, it works with the material which finds its way into the mind as a result of our environment, our contract with others, the sights we see, the sounds we hear and the like.

One of the most powerful principles of the mind is that known as Auto-Suggestion, through the aid of which we can continuously plant an idea in our own mind and concentrate upon it until it actually becomes a part of us to such an extent that it will dominate our actions and direct the movement of our bodies.

If you have enemies who are foolishly trying to undermine you, smile at them with tolerance and watch them tumble into the pitfalls which they dug for you.

Another characteristic of the human mind is the fact that it becomes a sort of magnet or lodestone which attracts to us other people who think, believe and act as we do. The human mind has a strong tendency to reach out and form affinities with other minds with which it is in harmony on one or more subjects.

Throughout the universe there is a law through the operation of which "like attracts like." This law is seen in operation quite readily in the manner in which one mind will attract to it other minds which harmonize with it.

If this is a true statement, and we know that it is, can you not see what a powerful force this law is, and can you not see what a tremendous aid it can be to you if you will cultivate and constructively use it?

The human mind seeks its level just as surely as water seeks its level, and it will not be content until it finds its level. We see this working out in the mind of the man of literary tastes and tendencies who seeks the companionship of similar minds; in the wealthy man who seeks companionship of the wealthy, and the poor man, who seeks the company of the poor.

If it were not for this law an oak tree never could spring from the acorn, because the atoms out of which the oak tree grows never would be attracted to one center in sufficient number to build that tree.

If it were not for this law, the human body never would mature, for the reason that the chemicals, food and nourishment would never be attracted and distributed to the proper places for growth and expansion.

If it were not for this law the material out of which finger nails are built would be distributed to the roots of the hair, or, to some other part of the body where not needed.

This law is as immutable as the law of gravitation which holds this earth in its course and keeps every planet of the universe in its proper place.

Analyze your friends. If you are not proud of them it is no particular credit to yourself because *you* are the magnet which has attracted them. The color and tendency of *your* mind is the attraction which has gathered around you other minds which harmonize with your own. If you do not like those who have been attracted to you, change the magnet which attracted them and pick up another set of friends.

A mighty fine way to magnetize your mind so it will attract to you the highest standard of human beings, is to set up in your mind an ideal that is patterned after men whom you most admire.

The modus operandi through which this is done is very simple, and *very effective!* You can even draw on the character of sundry other people for material out of which to build, in your mind, this ideal which is to become the magnet that will attract to you those who harmonize with it.

For example, take from the life of Washington those qualities which you most admired in him; from Lincoln those qualities which you most admired in him; from Jefferson those qualities which you most admired in him; from Emerson those qualities which you most admired in him, and so on down the line. Out of the composite of these qualities build an ideal–in other words, see yourself possessing all of these qualities, permitting no act or thought to pass which does not harmonize with this ideal–and the first thing you know you'll begin to resemble this ideal, and, more important still, *you will commence to attract to you others who harmonize with this ideal, either in whole or in part.*

Time is a perfect healer of mistakes, failures and grievances. If you've tried and failed, wait! Time will turn the wheel of fate around to success again, if you keep faith in self.

This is no mere theory. This writer knows that the plan works, because,–well, because of the only reason that anyone knows anything, for sure–he has tried it himself!

You place the material in your mind and the Great Unseen Alchemist works it into shape, building you a character and a personality which corresponds *exactly* to the nature of the material that you supply.

You now know how to gather the material!

You know how to be exactly what you want to be, and this writer will assume full responsibility for the soundness of this principle. It will work so that you, or even the most inexperienced unbeliever can see that it works in time, ranging all the way from a few hours to a few months, depending upon the extent to which you concentrate your mind upon the task, the extent to which you see *clearly* the picture of the ideal or the person you are building, etc.

This is Auto-Suggestion of which we are writing!

It is the principle through which you can build yourself over, or, through which you can build yourself to order. Through this principle you can master discouragement, worry, fear, hatred, anger, lack of self-control and the remainder of that long string of negative qualities which stand between most people and the full, happy, joyous life which is their right and heritage. These qualities are the weeds which correspond to those which spring up in the fertile soil of the fields when those fields are not plowed, cultivated and tilled.

This is not a new brand of religion of which you are reading; it is not a fad; it is not the outburst of an unbalanced, fanatical mind. It is a sound, scientific fact which any professor of psychology will corroborate.

These are just a few of the more elementary principles of your mind, stated in words which we intend to be so simple that a schoolboy or girl can understand them. For a more detailed study of that wonderful machine you carry around in your head go to the library, or to some good book store and buy a few books on Applied Psychology.

The only thing about you or anyone else that is really worthwhile is the *mind!* These old bodies that we carry around with us do not amount to much. They are merely the tools through which the mind operates, anyway. They cannot move an inch until the mind directs them to do so. If you would understand yourself, first learn something about your mind, and when you have learned a great deal about *your* mind *you* will know a great deal about *all minds,* because they all work in exactly the same manner.

BILLBOARD 11

CONCENTRATION

The eleventh billboard on the road to success is *concentration.*

Fifteen years ago this writer read "Graustark," by George Barr McCutcheon, for the first time. We began early in the evening and read all night. Next morning we were as fresh as if we had slept. To no extent were we fatigued. Furthermore, we remember the story of Graustark so clearly that we could relate it today as well as we could have done the day after reading it.

In later years, when we were studying law, we sat up many a night for a couple of hours, doing our best to keep awake while reading Greenleaf on Evidence and Blackstone's Commentaries. Two hours of that reading was about all we could stand at one sitting, and, strange enough, we did not remember very much of that which we read, even until the next day.

What was the difference between the two kinds of reading?

The difference was just this: In the first instance the story was told in absorbing, interesting style which caused the mind to become alert and to open itself to receive all that was read. In the second instance, the reading was dull and dry, the story was told in phrases which did not vibrate with life and action, consequently there was nothing to arouse the mind and prepare it to receive and record that which was read.

The human mind might be likened to a sponge. You know that a dry sponge will not absorb water readily. It must be held under the water and given time to become saturated before it will pick up its capacity quickly. So it is with the human mind. It must be aroused or it will not grasp the sense impressions which are coming in over the five senses of hearing, smelling, tasting, seeing and feeling.

Froebel discovered this principle when he invented the kindergarten system of teaching little children to learn by arousing their minds and intensifying their interest through play.

If you want to become the leading *teacher* in your school find ways and means of directing the minds of your students toward study through play. Get their minds aroused over the subject at hand and they will master that subject in much less time and to an extent which would not be otherwise possible.

If you are the foreman, with men and women under your supervision, find ways and means of arousing their minds, of interesting them in the task at hand, of getting them to love the work they are doing, and you will become noted for the efficiency of your workers. Work out ways and means of stimulating interest through competition, allowing bonuses to the worker or workers who perform a given task in less time than another worker or group of workers. These bonuses may be in the nature of extra compensation, promotion to higher work, off time, prizes, certificate of efficiency, or anything else which seems most appropriate for the class of workers you are dealing with.

Every efficient man who employs others knows that it is not a mere matter of charity, sentimentality or idealism to give his workers to clean, cheerful environment in which to work, but it is strictly sound business judgment.

Dairymen have learned that cows will give more milk when kept in clean stalls and kept free from annoyance by flies and other pests. Every doctor knows that a mother with a nursing baby at her breast cannot properly nourish the little fellow if she is in a state of worry and anxiety all the time, no matter how much food she, herself, may take.

The human mind, when brooding over troubles, manufactures and throws into the blood the most deadly of poisons, and if this goes on long enough it overtaxes the capacity of the purifying process of the liver and disease of almost any kind is apt to break out in the body.

Happiness, health, joy, the capacity to retain the sense impressions and to recall them at will, all have their seat or cause in the human mind. A peculiar thing about the mind is the fact that our bodily actions take on the form and color of our thoughts. Show me what a person thinks about most and I will very accurately analyze that person's actions for you. You cannot think of misery, suffering, poverty and disease and be prosperous, healthy and happy. These combinations simply do not make agreeable bed-fellows.

When Shakespeare wrote: "To thine own self be true, and it must follow, as the night the day, that thou canst not then be false to any man," he merely meant that we couldn't go wrong if we followed the promptings of our own conscience.

The time is coming when every place where men and women work will be equipped with appropriate play grounds and apparatus with which to coax the human mind into a harmonious state every few hours. There will be periods off for play, exercise and recuperation. Then you will have less use for your hospitals, jails and insane asylums. The human body, like the locomotive engine, must have attention, rest, repair and overhauling. Where on earth will you find a piece of machinery that will stand nearly every sort of abuse and lack of attention as long as the human body will stand it without going to pieces?

May it not be possible that some of the inventive genius of the world would find it profitable to itself and extremely valuable to the human race, to turn some of its effort toward the discovery of ways and means of artificially stimulating the human mind and arousing it so that it will become more alert, and so it will learn to switch from negative, destructive thoughts of worry, fear and anxiety, to positive, creative thought of courage, enthusiasm and good cheer.

Froebel, the inventor of the kindergarten, only scratched

the surface of the possibilities which are open to the educators of the present age. It took Froebel's system nearly a hundred years to gain momentum and popularity. If an educator or anyone else will take the concepts hinted at in this editorial and build them into a system through which adults as well as children may turn work into play, this writer will put that person on the world map in much less time. The columns of this magazine are available to every person who will invent ways and means of helping people overcome the fallacies and superstitions which have dogged the footsteps of the human race as relics of the stone age.

Anything which will cause people to think constructive thoughts is desirable. Anything which will cause the human race to become free thinkers and throw off dogmas and creeds is desirable. Of course, the moment you throw off your dogmatic chains and quit believing a thing merely because someone else told you to believe it, you automatically kill off that crop of human parasites who, like leeches, fatten on your ignorance and superstition. These little leeches will not want to see you become a free thinker, because the moment you do so you will quit paying them tribute. Generally speaking, any man who sets himself up as the last word of authority on a given subject is a menace to the process of the human race, a usurper of rights which the Creator probably never intended to relegate to him.

Usually these chaps who set themselves up as self-styled privileged leaders, claiming the power to lead the world or any part of it out of darkness into light, are nothing more or less than fanatics on one subject or another, and more often than otherwise, on all subjects.

One thing you will do well to think about, brother, is the fact that only that which you do for yourself, only the thinking which you and the conclusions which you reach in your own mind, will be of permanent value to you. Happiness is something which you cannot buy, "borrow," beg or steal. You have to create it in your own mind, and you cannot do this until you commence to study your own mind and understand it.

The best place to start studying the mind and the wonders which you can perform with yours, is with the simple concepts which we have mentioned. When you see for yourself that your body can perform twice as much work, and with less fatigue, when engaged in labor which you enjoy, as it can when you are engaged in work which you dislike, you will see that here is a principle which offers great possibilities. You will see that it pays to find the work into which you can throw your whole heart and soul; work which you will like. You will see that this principle offers great possibilities to the man who employs others, because he can, through its operation, increase their efficiency and add to their enjoyment of life, their earning capacity.

Less rhetoric and more results!

You are constantly building your character out of the impressions you gather from your daily environment, therefore you can shape your character as you wish. If you would build it strongly, surround yourself with the pictures of the great men and women you most admire; hang mottoes of positive affirmation on the walls of your room; place the books of your favorite authors on the table where you can get to them often, and read those books with pencil in hand, marking the lines which bring you the noblest thoughts; fill your mind with the biggest and noblest and most elevating thoughts, and soon you will begin to see your own character taking on the hue and color of this environment which you have created for yourself.

Mind Unfathomed Mine

What do you KNOW about your own mind? What do you know about any other mind? An old lady had been bed-ridden for twelve years, unable to turn over without help. Came to that home one day a man who understood a little, but not very much perhaps, about the strength of the human mind. He gathered the old lady's relatives around him and promised to cure her if they would all arrange to leave the house and let the old lady know that she was absolutely alone. After they had all cleared out this man slipped into the room, unnoticed, and set fire to the old lady's bed. With a scream and a single leap she gathered her wraps about her and ran from that room as though nothing were wrong with her. From that day on she remained out of bed. She was bed-ridden nowhere except in her own mind, the self–same place where most of us remain in poverty and failure and grief.

Learn How to Use That Wonderful Mind of Yours

The human mind is a composite of many qualities and tendencies. It consists of likes and dislikes, optimism and pessimism, hatred and love, constructiveness and destructiveness, kindness and cruelty. The mind is made up of all these qualities and more. It is a blending of them all, some minds showing one of these qualities dominating and other minds showing others dominating.

The dominating qualities are largely determined by one's environment, training, associates and particularly by one's own *thoughts!* Any thought held constantly in the mind, or any thought dwelt upon through concentration and brought into the conscious mind often attracts to it those qualities of the human mind which it most resembles.

A thought is like a seed planted in the ground in that it brings back a crop after its kind, multiplies and grows, therefore, it is dangerous to allow the mind to hold any thought which is destructive. Such thoughts must sooner or later seek release through physical action.

Through the principle of Auto Suggestion–that is, thoughts held in the mind and concentrated upon–any thought will soon begin to crystallize into action.

If the principle of Auto Suggestion were generally understood and taught in the public schools it would change the whole moral and economic standards of the world inside of twenty years. Through this principle the human mind can rid itself of its destructive tendencies by constantly dwelling upon its constructive tendencies. The qualities of the human mind need the sunlight of nourishment and use to keep them alive. Throughout the universe there is a Law of Nourishment and Use which applies to everything that lives and grows. This Law has decreed that every living thing which is neither nourished nor used must die, and this applies to the qualities of the human mind which we have mentioned.

The only way to develop any quality of the mind is to concentrate upon it, think about it and use it. Evil tendencies of the mind can be blotted out by starving them to death through *disuse!*

What would it be worth to the young, plastic mind of the child to understand this principle and commence to make use of it early in life, beginning with the kindergarten?

The Principle of Auto Suggestion is one of the fundamental major laws of Applied Psychology. Through a proper understanding of this principle and with the co-operation of the writers, philosophers, school teachers and preachers, the whole tendency of the human mind can be directed toward constructive effort inside of twenty years or less.

What are *you* going to do about it?

May it not be a good plan, as far as you are concerned individually, not to wait for someone to start a movement for general education along this line, but commence now to make use of this Principle for the benefit of you and yours?

Your children may not be fortunate enough to receive this training in school, but there is nothing to hinder you from giving it to them in your home.

You may have been unfortunate in that you never had an opportunity to study and understand the Principle of Auto Suggestion when you were going to school, but there is nothing to hinder you from studying, understanding and applying to your own efforts this principle from now on.

You will find a complete course in Applied Psychology running serially in this magazine. It began with the January issue. Go back to the beginning and read this course. It is written in understandable, simple language which any layman can absorb and apply.

Learn something about that wonderful machine which we call the human mind. It is your real source of power. If you ever free yourself of petty worries and financial want it will be through the efforts of that wonderful mind of yours.

Your editor is still a young man, yet he has positive evidence in many thousand cases of the transformation of both men and women from failure to success in remarkably short periods of time, ranging all the way from a few hours to a few months.

The magazine you hold in your hands is concrete evidence of the soundness of the argument that the individual can control his economic destiny, because it is a success which was built out of fifteen years of failure!

You can turn your past failure into success if you will understand and intelligently apply the principles of Applied Psychology. You can get to wherever you wish to go in life. You can find happiness instantly, once you master this principle, and you can build financial success as rapidly as you comply with the established practices and principles of economics.

There is nothing that savors of occultism in the human mind. It functions in harmony with the physical and economic laws and principles. You do not need the assistance of any person on earth in the manipulation of your own mind so it will function as you want it to. Your mind is something which *you* control, no matter what your station in life may be, provided always that you exercise that right instead of permitting others to do so for you.

Learn something of the powers of your mind. It will free you of the curse of fear and fill you with inspiration and courage.

BILLBOARD 12

PERSISTENCE

The twelfth billboard on the road of success is *persistence.*

We have made an important discovery—a discovery which may help you, whoever you are, whatever may be your aim in life, to achieve success.

It is not the touch of genius, with which some men are supposed to be gifted, which brings success!

It is not good luck, pull nor wealth!

The real thing upon which most great fortunes were built—the thing which helps men and women rise to fame and high position in the world—is easily described:

It is simply the habit of completing everything one begins, first having learned what to begin and what not to begin.

Take inventory of yourself covering the past two years, let us say, and what do we discover?

The chances are about fifty to one that we will discover that you have had many ideas, started many plans, but completed none of them!

In the series of lessons on Applied Psychology which are running serially in this magazine you will find one explaining the importance of *Concentration,* followed with simple, explicit information on exactly how to learn to concentrate.

You will do well to look that particular lesson up and study it over again—study it with a new idea in mind; that of learning how to complete all that you undertake.

You have heard it stated in axiomatic phraseology ever since you were old enough to remember, that "procrastination is the thief of time!" but because it seemed like a preachment you paid no heed to it.

That axiom is literally true!

You cannot possibly succeed in any undertaking, whether it is large or small, important or otherwise, if you merely think of that which you would like to accomplish and then sit down and wait for the thing to materialize without patient, painstaking effort!

Nearly every business which stands out prominently above the common run of similar business, represents concentration on a definite plan, or idea, from which there has been but little, if any, variance.

The United Cigar Stores merchandising plan is built upon an idea, simple enough, but upon which concentrated effort has been directed.

The Piggly-Wiggly retail stores were built upon a definite plan, through the principle of concentration, the plan itself being simple and easy of application to other lines of business.

The Rexal Drug Stores were built upon a plan, through the aid of concentration.

The Ford automobile business is nothing more than concentration upon a simple plan, the plan being to give the public a small, serviceable car for as little money as possible, giving the buyer the advantage of quantity production. This plan has not been materially changed in the last twelve years.

The great Montgomery Ward & Company and Sears, Roebuck & Company mail order houses represent two of the largest merchandising enterprises in the world, both having been built upon the simple plan of giving the buyer the advantage of quantity buying and selling, and, the policy of "satisfying" the customer or giving him his money back.

Both of these great merchandising concerns stand out as mammoth monuments to the principle of sticking to a definite plan, through concentration.

There are other examples of great merchandising success which were built upon the same principle, by adopting a definite plan and then *sticking to it to the end!*

However, for every great success to which we can point, as a result of this principle, we can find a thousand failures or *near failures* where no such plan has been adopted.

This writer was talking to a man a few hours before writing this editorial–a man who is a bright, and, in many ways a capable business man, but he is not succeeding for the simple reason that he has too many half-baked ideas and follows the practice of discarding all of them before they have been fairly tested.

This writer offered him a suggestion which might have been valuable to him, but he replied immediately–"oh, I've thought of that several times, and I started to try it out once, but it didn't work."

Note the words well:

*** "I started to try it out once, but it didn't work."

Ah, there was where the weakness might have been discovered. He "started" to try it out.

Reader of the Golden Rule, mark these words: *It is not the man who merely "starts" a thing who succeeds! It is the fellow who starts and who finishes in spite of hell!*

Anybody can start a task. It takes the so-called genius to muster up enough courage, self-confidence and painstaking patience to *finish* that which he starts.

But this is not "genius;" it is nothing *but persistence* and good, common sense. The man who is accredited with being a genius usually is, as Edison has so often told us, nothing of the kind–he is merely a hard worker who finds a sound plan and then sticks to it.

Success rarely, if ever, comes all in a bunch, or in a hurry. Worth-while achievement usually represents long and patient service.

Remember the sturdy oak tree! It does not grow in a year nor in two nor even three years. It requires a score of years or more to produce a fair-sized oak tree. There are trees which will grow very large in a few years, but their wood is soft and porous and they are short-lived trees.

The man who decides to be a shoe-salesman this year, then changes his mind and tries farming the next year, and then switches again to selling life insurance the third year is more than apt to be a failure at all three, whereas, had he stuck to one of these for three years he might have built a very fair success.

You see I know a great deal about that which I am writing because I made this same mistake for almost fifteen years. I feel that I have a perfectly good right to warn you of an evil which may be set your pathway because I have suffered many defeats on account of that evil and, consequently, I have learned how to recognize it in you.

The first of January–the day for good resolutions–is nearing. Set aside that day for two purposes and you will be quite likely to profit by having read this editorial.

First: Adopt a Chief Aim for yourself for the next year at least, and preferably for the next five years, and write out that aim word by word.

Second: Determine to make the first plank in that Chief Aim platform read something after this fashion: *"During the ensuing year I will determine as nearly as possible those tasks which I shall have to perform from start to finish in order to succeed, and nothing under the sun shall divert my efforts from finishing every task which I begin."*

Nearly every man has intelligence enough to create ideas in his mind, but the trouble with most men is that those ideas never find expression in *Action!*

The finest locomotive on earth is not worth a shilling, nor will it pull a single pound of weight until the stored up energy in the steam dome is released at the throttle!

You have energy in that head of yours–every normal human being has–but you are not releasing it at the throttle of *Action!* You are not applying it, through the principle of *concentration,* to the tasks which, if completed, would place you on the list of those who are regarded as successes.

As far as this writer can determine, the chief objection to

cigarettes is the indisputable fact that they have a very decided tendency to render the human mind "dopey" and *inactive!* This is enough to condemn them, because anything which retards a man's action, or the releasing of his ability through the habit of concentrating his mind upon a task until it is *finished,* is detrimental to his welfare.

Usually a man will release that flow of *action* which he has stored up in his head, in connection with a task which he delights in performing. That is the reason why a man ought to engage in the work which he likes best.

There is a way of coaxing that wonderful mind of yours to give up its energy and pour it out into action through concentration upon some useful work. Keep on searching until you find the best possible way of releasing this energy. Find the work through which you can release this energy most readily and most *willingly* and you will be getting mighty near to the work in which you ought to find success.

It has been this writer's privilege to interview many so-called great men—men who were regarded as "geniuses," and as a means of encouragement to you I want to tell you frankly that I found nothing in them which lows do not possess. They were exactly like us, with no more brains—sometimes with less—but what they had which you and I also have, *but do not always use,* was the ability to release the *action* which is stored up in their heads and keep it concentrated upon a task, great or small, until *completed.*

Do not expect to become an adept at concentration the first time you try. Learn first to concentrate upon the little things you do—the sharpening of a pencil, the wrapping of a package, the addressing of a letter, and so forth.

The way to attain perfection in this wonderful art of finishing all that you start, is to form the habit of doing this in connection with every task you perform, no matter how small. The first thing you know this becomes a regular habit and you do it automatically, without effort.

Of what importance will this be to you?

What a useless, silly question—but listen and we shall answer:

It will mean the difference between failure and success!

BILLBOARD 13

LEARNING FROM FAILURE

The thirteenth billboard on the road to success is *learning from failure.*

The Man Who Fails!

"Oh, men, who are labeled 'failures'—up, rise up! again and do!
Somewhere in the world of action is room; there is room for you.
No failure was e'er recorded, in the annals of truthful men,
Except of the craven-hearted who fails, nor attempts again.
The glory is in the doing, and not in the trophy won;
The walls that are laid in darkness may laugh to the kiss of the sun.
Oh, weary and worn and stricken, oh, child of fate's cruel gales!
I sing,—that it haply may cheer him,—I sing to the man who fails."

There need be no permanent failure. Every reverse and every set back can be turned into a building stone for a solid foundation of success.

Failures teach us to be tolerant. Failures teach us to be persistent. There is a great lesson in every failure, even though we may not, for the time being, know what it is.

I sometimes think that failure is nature's tempering process through which she prepares men of destiny for their responsibilities.

If you can survive repeated failures instead of going down before them it is strong evidence that you will rise to the heights in your chosen life work.

Don't despise failures—thank God for the privilege of testing yourself under their weight!

"All honor to him who shall win the prize,
The world has cried for a thousand years,
But to him who tries and who fails and dies,
I give great honor and glory and tears.
And great is the man with a sword undrawn,
And good is the man who refrains from wine
But the man who fails and yet still fights on,
Lo, he is the twin-brother of mine."

Handicaps—Physical and Mental

There are two kinds of handicaps. One is mental and the other merely physical. The latter should not worry us very much, where there is a strong, sound mind, even though that mind may be latent and undeveloped.

During the western lap of my recent speaking tour I met a man very much worth knowing. I had ridden in an automobile with him for several miles and talked with him for nearly three hours before I discovered that he was blind.

He wore dark colored glasses, but outside of this there was nothing in his speech or manner to indicate any such affliction as blindness, which belongs under the heading of physical handicaps.

But this man was by no means handicapped mentally. He is one of the most fluent talkers I ever listened to, and he possesses that very rare ability to talk about subjects which cause one to think, analyze and synthesize.

The man of whom I write is Reverend Wilmore Kendall, pastor of the Methodist Church at Lawton, Oklahoma.

Dr. Kendall has been blind since he was a couple of years old. Some years ago he presented himself at the Northwestern University in Chicago, for matriculation. They looked at him with surprise, and when he said he had only $35.00 with which to pay his way through, they commenced to believe something was wrong with him!

And, something was!

What a pity that same "something" is not wrong with more people. The university refused to permit him to enroll. He walked around the block a time or two, thought out a plan, then came back and asked them to give him just three months' trial and if he did not make good they could throw him out.

More out of sympathy than anything else, they gave him this trial, never expecting, of course, that he could possibly do the work and stick.

But he fooled'em!

He went through that term and through the terms that followed until he got his degree. And how do you suppose he managed to pay the expense of that training?

Grip the arms of your chair firmly, and get ready for a shock, you fellows who howl, whine and rail at fate for "not giving you a chance"–he paid his way by taking notes of the lectures, transcribing them and selling them to the other students.

By the eternal here is a man whom some of the rest of us would do well to emulate. If we had his self-confidence, determination, power of concentration and will power we could rise to whatever position in life we might aim for, and we may have these in *exactly the same way that he acquired his!*

The following news item, clipped from a daily newspaper, tells of another case of physical handicap which in no way interfered with success:

Years ago a 15-year-old boy fell under a train up in the copper country. He came out of the hospital penniless. His legs below the knees were gone. So was his left arm. His right hand was only a stump. There seemed no place to go but the poorhouse; nothing to look forward to but a grave in the potter's field.

No man can have perfect faith in God and still lack self-confidence, a truth which becomes increasingly plain as time passes and the human mind begins to unfold itself.

Yesterday Michael J. Dowling, president of the Minnesota Bankers' Association, candidate for governor of the state, told how the boy cheated both poorhouse and potter's field. For Mr. Dowling was the crippled boy grown up—successful. Supported by artificial legs, his left coat sleeve filled by an artificial arm, he voiced his philosophy to the Association of Commerce at its noonday luncheon in the Hotel La Salle:

"The only permanently helpless cripple is the man with a crippled head," Mr. Dowling said. "And in my travels I have found more permanent cripples—otherwise able bodied—than can be found among those who have physical handicaps. The man who has lost arms, legs, or eyes can be a useful member of society if he is given a chance to fit himself for work, his physical handicap does not prohibit his performing. There is no reason why such a man should not marry and be the center and support of a happy family. Wooden legs and arms are not inherited—only wooden heads are passed from generation to generation. I have three daughters—there's no wood in their anatomy. I have been reasonably successful. There is no reason why any cripple whose heart and head are right should not succeed."

Mr. Dowling is right—"the only permanently helpless cripple is the man with a crippled head." I know of no remedy for that. But many suffer from lack of mental development who could succeed if they should discover the possibilities within their minds.

If you have lost an arm or two, or even both legs and both arms, there is still plenty for you to do in the world if you have not lost your grip on yourself mentally.

I am firmly of the opinion that I could get along without the use of my legs, arms, and even my eyes, if my mind were left intact and my tongue were left free to talk to my "Ediphone."

I feel mightily ashamed when I think of Reverend Kendall, of Lawton, Oklahoma. Without the use of his eyes he is doing and has done so much good in the world, and with the full use of my eyes and all other physical faculties, I have accomplished so little.

When you feel inclined to pity yourself, go out and look up a man like Kendall, and get a good injection of "pep" from him. It will do you good.

Alibi Builders

One of the commonest of mistakes is that of finding an excuse or creating an alibi to explain the reason why we do not succeed.

This would be just the thing if it were not for the universal tendency to look every place except the right place for this excuse, which is in the nearest looking glass.

Last year we had a man on our staff who had the very best sort of reason for all that *he did not accomplish.*

He is not with us any longer!

He gravitated on and out, joining the ranks of those untold millions which constitute 95 percent of the people of the world–the fellows who *do not succeed.*

If you asked him his side of the story he would undoubtedly say there was nothing wrong with *him;* his trouble was that this magazine did not appreciate a fine fellow like him!

It takes a courageous man–a big, manly man–an honest man–to look himself squarely in the face and say, "I am looking at the fellow who is standing between me and success–get out of the way so I can pass!" We haven't many such persons, but wherever you find one you find a man who is doing worthwhile things, who is serving the world constructively and usefully.

It may give one a certain amount of satisfaction to charge others with his failure, and with his poor lot in life, but this practice surely does not tend to improve one's station in life.

I ought to know, for I must confess that I have tried it just enough in my time to find out that it will not work!

I have in mind a very dear friend who works rather closely to me in the business world. I know him well enough to feel privileged to tell him just what I believe to be his chief handicaps, but up to the present the only results have been to hear him find a fault with me to match every one that I find in him.

And, perhaps, he is right; perhaps I have more faults than he has, *but the big point that I want the readers of these lines to get, remember and make use of is this: It makes no difference what faults this chap may find in me or in others, he will sink or swim, rise, or fall, on his own merits, and unless he quits building alibis and goes to building character, by looking himself squarely in the face, he will wind up just where all alibi builders end, in the scrap heap of failure!*

We all love to be flattered, but none of us love to hear the truth about our faults. Some flattery is a mighty fine thing. It urges us on to undertake more, but too much of it causes us to lapse into inertia.

If I had no enemies it would be necessary for me to go out and punch my finger in someone's eye and make a few, because I need someone to keep me on the jump; to keep me from becoming self-satisfied; to keep me on the defensive in one way or another. When I am defending myself I am growing stronger, developing my strategic ability and keeping in fighting trim so that when I need to fight I will know how to fight.

It will do you no good to spend time looking for faults in those whom you do not like, or in those who have been courageous enough to point out yours to you, or in those who have outdistanced you in the game of life and are succeeding while you have failed. They have faults, make no mistake about that, but the time you spend proving that they have faults is time wasted, because you can make no use of this proof after you get it. Better by far that you spend this time checking up yourself to find out why you have not succeeded and how you may eliminate those faults which have been pointed out to you.

You will not enjoy this as much as you would enjoy the applause of indulgent, admiring friends, but it will do you a site more good in the long run.

The Way of Success Is the Way of Struggle!

I come back, once more, to claim your attention for a few minutes on a subject which has made a tremendous impression on my mind during the past few years.

The conclusions which I have reached have been the only ones that a man with an open mind could have reached. I have seen so much evidence of the soundness of the principle which I shall pass on to you, once more, that I can recommend it to you as being worthy of your earnest consideration.

If a brick could talk no doubt it would complain when it is placed in a red hot kiln and burned for hours; yet, that process is necessary in order to give the brick lasting qualities that will withstand the onslaught of the elements.

The prize-fighter must take a great deal of punishment before his is ready to step into the ring and meet an adversary, yet, if he fails to take that punishment and prepare for the final battle, he is sure to pay with defeat.

My little son has just staggered into my study, with wobbly legs, and with tears in his eyes. He just received a hard fall a moment ago while trying to balance himself on those little legs. He is learning to walk. He would never walk if he did not get many a fall and keep on trying.

The eagle builds her nest far above the tops of the trees, on some rugged crag, in the cliffs, where no depredating man nor animal can reach her young. But, after taking all this precaution to protect her young, she will subject them to another danger just as soon as she believes they are ready to learn to fly. She will take them out to the edge of the rocks, push them over and *"make them fly."* Of course, she is right there to take the plunge with them, and if they are too weak to fly, she will dart under them, catch them in her claws, take them back to the nest and wait another day or so, then take them out again. This is the only way young eagles would learn to fly–*through struggle!*

It is more profitable to be an attentive listener than it is to be a fluent talker.

And, as time and experience begin to extend my vision into the silent workings of Nature, I cannot help seeing that there is a guiding hand which pushes us into struggle that we may emerge with more knowledge of the things which we need to know in life.

The Law of Compensation is relentless in its work of helping man rise higher and higher through struggle! An athlete becomes an athlete only by practice, training and struggle, just as a man becomes a doer only by *doing!* Some men learn easily and quickly, while Nature finds it necessary to break the hearts of others before they will recognize her handwriting on the walls of Time.

Back in my earlier days, before I had learned to read very much that Nature had written for my eyes, I often wondered when, where and how I would find myself; how I would know when I had come to myself; how I would know when I had found my life work!

I suspect that this has worried many another!

To all such persons I bring a message of assurance and hope. You may be sure that as long as failure, heart-aches and adversities come your way, Nature is struggling with you, trying to swerve your course in life. She is trying to switch you off in the side track of failure onto the main line of success.

Read the above paragraph again!

When you are unhappy, unsuccessful, and in trouble, there is something wrong! These conditions of mind are Nature's guide-posts which point out to you that you are struggling in the wrong direction.

Make no mistake about this. Nature always points the way, and you *will know when you are traveling in the right direction, just as definitely as you know when you have placed you hand on a red hot stove.* If you are unhappy do not overlook the fact that this is an unnatural state of mind–that you have a right to happiness–and it is a sure sign *that there is something wrong in your life!*

Who ascertains what this "something" is that is wrong?

You do! Only you can do so!

A few souls–and they are rare indeed–follow Nature's guiding hand easily and readily. The Great Struggle with these people is not so painful. They respond readily when Nature touches them on the elbow with a stroke of adversity; but the majority of us have to be severely punished before we begin to realize that we are being punished.

The principles through which material, monetary success, for example, can be attained, are comparatively simple. They were laid down in the March issue of this magazine, under the heading of "The Great Magic Ladder to Success." There are sixteen rungs to this ladder and every one of them is simple and easy to attainment, but the price that must be paid in return for this attainment is struggle–struggle at every step upward.

Nothing is gained without something is given in return!

You may have whatever you want in this life if you will pay the price in struggle, sacrifice and intelligent effort. To this extent you can avail yourself of the power of the Law of Retaliation, a law through the application of which you *get* exactly that which you *give!*

When a stranger, or a man whose record you know not of, appears at the gates of your employment and asks you to submit to his leadership, it can do no harm if you at least take the trouble to compare him with the man at the head of the works, to see which seems to be the sounder leader.

Stop worrying and fretting over your troubles and adversities and thank the Creator that he wisely placed these guide-posts in your pathway to help you right yourself. The normal state of mind is happiness. Just as sure as the sun rises in the east and sets in the west, happiness will come to the person who has learned to change his course when he comes to the mile-posts of failure, adversity and remorse.

Most of us have heard of a certain word called "conscience," but few of us, indeed, have learned that this thing is a Master Alchemist, which can turn the dross and base metals of failure and adversity into the pure gold of Success.

But it is true! Not figuratively, but *literally.*

The harder your struggle seems, the more evidence you have that you need to be worked over.

When adversity, failure and discouragement seem to stare you in the face most unmercifully, let me give you this formula through which you can defeat these: *Change your attitude toward your fellow men and devote your entire efforts to the task of helping others find happiness. In your struggle, which is the price you must pay Nature in return for her work in transforming you, you will find happiness yourself.*

To get it you must first give it away!

Do not sneer at this simple, homely advice. It comes from one who has tried the formula, know it works, and therefore, has the right to speak authentically.

After you have found happiness; after you have mastered that thing which you call your "temper" and have learned how to look upon all of your fellow men with tolerance and compassion; after you have learned to sit down and calmly and serenely take inventory of your past, you will see, as clearly as you can see the sun on a bright day, that Nature has made you struggle as the only means of helping you find your way out of the darkness.

You will know, then, that you have found yourself. You will know, also, that struggle has its purpose in this life. You will know that the Creator took you out to the edge of the cliffs and pushed you over, just as the mother eagle pushed her young ones over, so you could learn to fly!

You will be at peace with all mankind, then, because you will see that the struggle which you had to make, as a result of opposition by your fellow men, was the training which you needed through which to find your place in the world. You will also see that *you* and not your fellow men were the cause for this struggle.

This probably is the finest editorial I ever wrote, yet, I feel sure that only those who have known what it is to struggle, who have known what it is to fail, who have seen success grow out of the worst sort of failure, will appreciate it for all it is worth!

The others will appreciate it further down the road, after they have met with adversity, failure and discouragement; after they have discovered, just as I have done, that struggle is Nature's way of training the wobbly, baby legs of mankind to walk.

Small Beginnings Make Large Endings

Out in the city of Lawton, Oklahoma, lives a man to whom I wish to direct your attention.

His name is J. Hale Edwards and he is President of the Lawton Business College.

Now, the thing that moves me to write this brief editorial is, that this man Edwards possesses certain qualities which you and I and every other person on earth must develop before we can succeed.

First of all, he knows that success cannot be attained without paying the price which success always demands. He knows that one cannot *get* unless one first *gives!*

But, of more important than this, he has learned the lesson which so many otherwise great souls never learn, that the big *successes* have little *beginnings!*

I went to Lawton to address the citizens of the city, at the Public Auditorium, under the auspices of Mr. Edwards' school. In that audience was as fine a crowd of people as it has ever been my pleasure to meet. Had I not met Mr. Edwards I could have told, from the audience which he had attracted, what sort of a character he was.

I had not seen his school until the day following my address.

Naturally I had expected to find a big, elaborate business school, such as may be found in almost any city the size of Lawton, with a big staff of teachers. Judging from the size and the quality of the audience which Mr. Edwards had attracted to listen to my address I would have imagined that his school, also, was large.

But it wasn't!

What it did not represent in quantity, I am convinced, however, it made up in *quality!*

The teaching staff consisted of Mr. Edwards and his wife.

The equipment was of plain, unvarnished lumber of the

home spun type, but, as far as I could see, it served the purpose just as well as though it had been made of pure gold.

If you cannot be President of the United States, reach out and claim the next HIGHEST place for yourself by engaging in some work which will help men to see the glory of being decent with one another.

I give these details, not as a reflection on the school equipment of my host, for, indeed, this would be poor taste, but, instead, as a compliment to his intelligence, to his perseverance, to his determination, and just as surely as you are reading these lines J. Hale Edwards will step right up front and take his place along with the larger and better equipped schools in record-breaking time.

The man who is willing to start at the bottom is a rare soul, but when you find him you may be sure he will climb to the top ahead of the fellow who starts further up the ladder.

There are larger schools than Mr. Edwards', but I doubt that they can give any better instruction than his school gives. In fact his plant has advantages which the larger one does not; he can give his students closer individual attention.

I know what can be done, even with humble equipment, because I took my first Business College work under a man who had two little rooms in a dwelling house, his entire equipment being enough to accommodate only about a dozen students.

On my desk is a manuscript offered to our magazine for publication. I recognized the name on that manuscript the moment I saw it. I first heard that name some twenty years ago. The fellow back of it referred to me as "that rube from the coal mines!" He was in college and I was working in the mines. We met and he thought it a shrewd thing to show me up as being out of his class.

Calmness of mind is one of the beautiful jewels of wisdom. It is the reward for long and patient self-control.

I have read the manuscript. It is full of splendid English—much better in fact, than I could write, but, *it lacks soul!* It does not carry a worthwhile thought. It resembles a glass of stale beer—there is no "kick" in it!

The fellow back of that manuscript did not begin low enough down the ladder. Some of that coal mine experience which he sought to plague me with would have been good for him, perhaps; I don't know! At any rate I do know that it never hurts one to begin down at the bottom. In fact I believe that it is the only safe place to begin. This is why I say, "keep your eyes on J. Hale Edwards of Lawton, Oklahoma, because he is *willing to begin at the bottom!*

The Most Remarkable Age in All History

Those who live in the present age ought to feel very fortunate, because this is the most progressive and the most interesting age of all history.

What a rich heritage man has fallen heir to within the experience of this writer, during the past thirty years.

We have seen the birth of the automobile, the flying machine, the telephone, the wireless telegraphy, the submarine (with its possibilities for constructive work in removing ores, fuel and other natural resources from under the sea), the x-ray, the typewriter and a myriad of other useful inventions which help man to harness and use the forces of the universe.

But, more wonderful than all of these mechanical contrivances has been the discovery of the human mind and its possibilities. We have commenced to discover how to overcome fear, worry, discouragement, and, the worst of all negative mental conditions, superstition. We have discovered that "nothing is so good or bad but thinking makes it so."

The human race is now experimenting with the human mind. In all great discoveries the unfoldment comes, first by experimentation, then by experience and practice. Soon we will understand a great deal about that wonderful machine called the human mind; then we shall take our next big step forward in the elimination of disease, hatred, disagreements between mankind and the other string of millstones which hang around the necks of humanity.

Those of us who have as many as fifty active years ahead of us may be prepared to see greater achievements within that time than we have seen during the past fifty. When the human mind begins to unfold itself things will begin to happen on this earth.

The new age which we are just entering, since the close of the world war, may properly be called the cycle of mental discovery. The one just ended, with the war, may be called the cycle of mechanical or physical discovery.

Evolution works in cycles! We have a period of material development and out of this comes a period of mental development. In the beginning of these cycles or periods of development we make foolish use of the tools placed at our disposal, often using them destructively. Just as the submarine was first used as a forerunner of death and will later be used as a tool of investigation and progress, so will we have our Ouija Boards and other fake mechanical contrivances through which to prevent much of that great unknown, uncharted mass of mental phenomena to destructive use during the beginning of this new cycle of mental development.

The way of success is the way of struggle. If the thing you acquired or the position you attained came without struggle, you may be sure it will not be permanent. Remember the oak tree and the gourd. One grew in a decade, the other in a season.

Let this disturb us not at all! The encouraging feature is the fact that we have actually commenced to study the possibilities of the human mind. We have our fakers, in this study, just as we have always had them; the fellows who will seize this opportunity to prey upon the credulousness of humanity; but gradually these will pass on and the Truth will stand resplendent in its own beauty, free of embellishments and trimmings placed on it by those who would prevent its use for personal gain.

We will have our Sir Oliver Lodge and our Conan Doyle, but they should disturb us not at all. These fellows feel it their privilege to sell fiction for a profit. We could hardly expect a man like Conan Doyle to produce anything outside of the field of pure fiction, considering the years he has spent in producing this sort of material, his Sherlock Holmes detective stories and the like. In producing these stories his mind was trained to live, not in the field of reality, but in the atmosphere of imagination.

Just as a person who tells a lie over and over, finally comes to believe it, so do these chaps who live in the field of imagination finally come to believe in their own yarns, spun out of the environment in which they have lived.

We cannot blame them for this, except insofar as their yarns mislead the credulous mind to its detriment, causing it to become unbalanced.

Truth will finally make such things impossible. We shall learn more about the possibilities of the human mind, and while I do not know for sure, yet, I strongly suspect that when we have gone to the bottom of our experimentation and discovery along this line we shall find that no one on this earth can do anything for us which we cannot do for ourselves. I suspect that we shall find that latent within our own minds are all the possibilities which we could find in other minds. I suspect that we shall find in our own minds all the power we will know how to use; all the power we shall need in this life.

The Eternal Law of Attraction

Some parents complain that their sons and daughters worry them by showing a tendency to stray away from home. Farmers complain that their children are attracted by the city.

The remedy is simple. Make the home more attractive than the outside and the sons and daughters will not want to run away from it. Too many "don'ts" will cause any boy or girl to seek outside companionship and gradually drift away from the home ties. If the boys and girls want music, let them have it. If they want to dance, encourage them to do so. Find out just what it is that attracts them away from home and then hold them at home by that attraction for them.

Restraint naturally makes a person want to cut the ties and get away, regardless of the nature of the restraint. The human mind rebels strongly against everything that is forced upon it. You get people to do things through the Law of Attraction–not the law of force.

The churches–some of them at least–are not as full as they might be. The ministers may complain, urge and coerce, but the more they do this the more empty will their church pews become. People will go to church only when they are attracted there. Make the church program as attractive as the moving picture show and the movies will have to close on Sunday nights.

People go to movies because the owners study what the human mind wants *and then supply it!* It pays to do this in any undertaking. Nothing is so profitable as the rendering of service or providing of amusement which people want!

Some children play truant and remain out of school, while others show no particular interest in what goes on while they are in the schoolroom. The remedy is simple. Make the educational system interesting. Make it entertaining as well as instructive and then you will *attract* the boys and girls to the schoolroom. They will show deeper interest and remember what takes place much longer.

It is always necessary to explain mistakes and failures, but success explains itself, therefore devote your time to building a success and you will not need to create an "alibi."

Husbands sometimes stray away from their wives when they get a chance, while still others deliberately create the opportunity to do so. How long will it take wives to learn of this Law of Attraction through the operation of which they can hold their husbands just as they did before marriage. A few wives understand this law, make themselves attractive and find no trouble in holding their husbands, but most wives have not made this discovery.

A few of the more progressive type of employers have discovered this law and are making practical use of it by making the workshop a pleasant place. Out in the great packing houses, in the Chicago stockyards, the packers have learned the value of a pleasant environment. Beautiful rest rooms are provided for the women workers. Dance halls with music have been provided, and everything is made attractive and inviting.

It is just a matter of time until employers will learn generally to provide working quarters which are as attractive, at least, as the quarters which they provide for their live stock. Farmers and dairymen are beginning to learn, the more progressive at least, that it pays in dollars and cents to make a cow's living quarters dry and pleasant. She will give more milk in this sort of an atmosphere.

One of these days, thanks to the intelligent co-operation of the Industrial Engineers, employers will understand the economic value of providing music for the lunch hour, attractive epigrams and wall cards carrying positive messages wherever a worker may cast his eyes, and supplying light refreshments in the middle of the forenoon and the middle of the afternoon, when the workman's interest is naturally beginning to wane.

During these hot days fifty cents worth of ice, fifty cents worth of lemons, a bucket of water, which is free, and a little sugar, made into lemonade and passed out from workman to workman, would be about as fine as investment as an employer could make. The project would even warrant the services of a boy to carry the bucket around to the men every hour or so, especially during the long, hot afternoons.

The most unintelligent sort of an employer would see to it his draft horses were properly watered, why not use the same intelligence in dealing with the man-power of his plant, which is far more important than his horse-power?

It would not be a bad idea for some feature film concern (or some other energetic Yankee, who knows a good idea when he hears of it) to put out a series of short movie films, depicting, let us say, the reward of loyalty, the benefit of industrious effort, the value of initiative and so on, to be shown during a fifteen minutes' recess in the middle of the afternoon. All who use this idea will do well to provide some sort of music, also, during the entertainment, being careful to pick music which is inspiring and which would send the men back to their work whistling or humming to the rhythm of some snappy song. That rhythm would carry the workers the remainder of the day and they would more than make up the fifteen or twenty minutes lost during the recess.

Make the workshop attractive. Understand this great Law of Attraction and apply it to your business, profession or home affairs.

Whenever you get another person to do something because he wants to do it, you are availing yourself of this law. This is really the best way to get anyone to do anything, because service rendered in response to this law is never begrudged or regretted.

A woman can have her husband arrested and forced to support her, but the better way is to attract him so he will want to do so without force.

The same applies to the children who show a tendency toward drifting away from home. There is something wrong in the home which does not attract and hold children. True, this "something" may be the children themselves, but if we go deeply enough in our analysis, I suspect we will find that the parents are to blame.

We parents do not like to hear this said of us when a boy or girl is "bad" and frolics off with other "wayward" boys and girls, but if we would face the music courageously we would have to admit its truth.

The professional gossip swears everyone to secrecy, and tips from office to office under pretense of being the friend of the man whose character and reputation and future he at heart desires to destroy.

—Bernard Meador

Tom Sawyer, Mark Twain's famous character, had the right "dope." Instead of bemoaning the fact that he was put to work whitewashing a broad fence, he made that work look so "attractive" to the boys of the neighborhood that he farmed the job out to them, *charging them so many green apples for the privilege of painting so many square feet.*

Anything that you impose upon your boy as a "penalty" will seem hard to him, and he will want to get out of it, no matter how attractive the job might actually be if presented from a different viewpoint.

All of which, summed up in a few words, may be expressed very concretely by the statement that human beings love to be attracted and hate to be forced to do anything.

Bill collectors would do well to learn something about this law; especially those whose business it is to collect from people who are "judgment proof," and who cannot be forced to pay. The remedy here is to "attract" them into wanting to pay.

When you learn to apply this great Law of Attraction you will be an able salesman, no matter what it is you have to sell, because you will have learned the rare art of persuasion—the art of getting a person to do a thing by showing its attractive side—by appealing to the self-interest motive of the buyer.

This is the warp and the woof of all scientific salesmanship, whether one is selling his personal services, goods and wares, professional services in the pulpit, law office or counting room, or selling himself to a prospective wife.

If your modus operandi contemplates the use of force instead of persuasion you are on the wrong track and the sooner you switch over the better off you will be. There are two ways of getting a person to do a thing. One is through coercion, force and the exercise of power; the other is through the Law of Attraction. If you do not now understand the difference in the two methods, nothing else we might say in this editorial could possibly be of aid to you.

P.S.—This came as an afterthought. It really was suggested by Mrs. Hill, who is my English critic and supplies not a few of the ideas which find their way into these editorials. She suggests that I remind employers that it might not be such a bad idea if they sat in the labor councils with their men and met with them from time to time to consider ways and means of making the workshop more attractive. She believes this might be a very good way of settling difficulties before they arise.

Men are going to organize anyway. They are going to listen to the most dominant figure in their midst. The way to defeat the labor leader who is not honest with his followers, and who is bleeding them and leading them astray in many instances, is to step right into the ranks of your men with a leader of your own who will hold out more attractive "bait."

Not such a bad idea, for a woman!

And this reminds me to add a few words to the effect that employers in many instances are directly responsible for the alienation of their workmen's loyalty because they make no attempt to lead them. Men will have leaders. If the men themselves don't discover this the *leaders do!* It makes a big difference to the employer who the leader is, what type of man he is, whether he is honest or dishonest, playing a square game with his followers or exploiting them. It also makes a big difference to the men themselves.

In some communities the principal diversion is pitching horseshoes and looking up the mistakes and the past life of a neighbor or an occasional visitor.

We suspect that the employer who, out of indifference or ignorance, permits an outside leader to come along and attract the loyalty of his men away from him, deserves no more than he gets.

It is no mere accident when men go on strike, become unreasonable, demand wages which are not being earned in profits by the employer and other things equally as impossible, as they sometimes do. It is, or should be, a part of the employer's business to keep his men informed on the capacity of the business to pay wages. Also, it is no mere accident that we find men in some places of employment who are happy, satisfied, industrious and loyal! Yes, there are such organizations, and there could be many more of them if employers would study this Law of Attraction a little more closely.

The Human Mind Will Not Tolerate "Forced" Control

Prune a tree and you strengthen its trunk and roots. Destroy the sense of hearing and the other four senses, or some of them, will be correspondingly increased. The Law of Compensation sees to it that nothing is destroyed.

You can burn a tree, but you cannot destroy that which composes it. Its elements will go back to their original source. You can turn water into steam, but you cannot destroy it. In time it goes back to its original state.

So it is with the human mind. It can be suppressed and controlled in some of its activities, but it will become correspondingly stronger in other directions.

Anything that is imposed upon the human mind, against its will, starts that mind to work endeavoring to find another outlet for its energy. This is a principle which lawmakers would do well to remember. The passing of kings, czars and kaisers is but the latest manifestation of this principle in operation.

The Imperial German Criminal Code of 1870 was signed by *Bismarck* and William I. The sedition sections quoted below were enforced against newspapers, labor organizations and Socialists with great severity by Bismarck. The result was unexpected. The Socialist party became the largest in Germany. And, in general, so much patriotic loyalty and devotion to the then form of government was generated that a harness maker is now president of German republic and Kaiser William II is studying windmills in Holland.

Sections from Imperial German Criminal Code–High Treason and Treason.

Sec. 81. Anyone who undertakes by force to alter the constitution of the German Empire or a federal state, or the succession to the crown established therefore *** shall be guilty of High Treason and be liable to Penal Internment or Military Detention for life. If there are extenuating circumstances the punishment shall be Military Detention for not less than *five years.*

Sec. 82. Any act directly tending to the carrying out of the intention shall be regarded as an undertaking by which the crime of High Treason is completed.

Sec. 83. If several persons have agreed upon the carrying out of a treasonable undertaking, but their conduct has not amounted to an offense under Section 82, they shall be liable to Penal Internment or Military Detention of not less than five years. If there are extenuating circumstances the punishment shall be Military Detention of *not less than two years.*

Sec. 85. Anyone who publicly before a crowd, or by declamation or public placarding or public display of writings or other representations, incites to the carrying out of an offense punishable under Section 82, shall be liable to Penal Internment or Military Detention not exceeding ten years. If there are extenuating circumstances the punishment shall be Military Detention of from *one to five years.*

Chapter II. Insulting a Reigning Prince.

Sec. 95. Anyone who insults the Kaiser, his reigning prince, or during his residence in the federal state its reigning prince, shall be liable to confinement of not less than two months or of Military Detention of from *two months to five years.*

Sec. 97. Anyone who insults a member of the Reigning House or the Regent Prince of his state *** shall be liable to confinement or Military Detention of from *one month to three years.*

Chapter III. Opposition to Public Authority.

Sec. 110. Anyone who in public and in the presence of a number of persons or by the circulation of statements, the public exhibition of placards or the public distribution of written documents or other representations, incites to disobedience of law or any lawful proclamation or an order made by a competent authority, shall be liable to a fine not exceeding six hundred marks or to confinement *not exceeding two years.*

Sec. 111. Anyone who incites in the manner aforesaid the commission of a punishable act, *if a punishable act or attempt results therefrom,* be similarly liable as an instigator. *If there is no such result,* the punishment shall be a fine not exceeding *one year.* In no case, however, shall the punishment exceed that laid down for the act itself.

You are a composite of the words you speak, the literature you read, the thoughts you harbor, the company you keep and the station in life to which you aspire.

It is to be noted that the Kaiser's punishments were not so severe as those meted out by American judges in 1919.

Verily, it is written in the Scriptures, that he who lives by the sword will die by the sword!

This applies to you and I, as individuals, just the same as to kings, czars and kaisers. We can foretell what our finish will be by analyzing what we are now in our dealings with our fellow men.

This is no mere preachment! You have heard it before, it is true, but possibly you have not thought seriously that it applied to you. The ex-kaiser, perhaps, made the same mistake.

"Whatsoever a man soweth, that shall be also reap."

There is no escape from this Law. It is as broad as the universe. It governs every person on earth. We can sometimes get around man-made laws, but this eternal Law of Compensation, *never!*

Back of this law we may find the *real reason* why "it pays to be honest."

We may fool ourselves into believing that we are getting by this law, and, for a time it may appear that we are evading it, but eventually it rounds us up and forces an accounting.

A little dishonestly and a little experience in lying is good for a person. They act as their own witness and present their own proof that they will not work.

Control of steam has been a mighty fine thing for the human race, because it has lightened man's burdens and aided in man's progress, but control of the human mind is another matter.

The one and only true method of controlling the human mind is that which is self-imposed, through the aid of education!

Educate the human race; teach men and women the *whys* and the *wherefores* of these eternal truths that we have been presenting in axiomatic form and in mere preachments; let people know *why* it "pays to be honest"; why it pays to be decent with one's fellow men; why the outward acts of humanity correspond exactly to the nature of the thoughts which dominate the human mind, and human beings will need less controlling. They will learn *how to control themselves,* just as the more intelligent of the human race are doing now.

Enough scientific knowledge has been passed on through the pages of this magazine since its birth, in 1918, to change the entire trend of the human race in a single generation if it were systematically taught in the public schools. There was enough sound instruction in "The Great Magic Ladder to Success," in the March, 1920, issue, to so change the attitude of man toward man in a single generation that jailhouses and penitentiaries could be torn down, or turned into asylums for the treatment of those who grew up in ignorance of these principles.

This is no mere bouquet that we are handing to ourselves. It is a conservative statement of a possibility, and we shamefully admit it.

BILLBOARD 14

TOLERANCE

The fourteenth billboard on the road to success is *tolerance.*

There are three powers which, if properly organized, could change the entire customs of the world in a single generation!

If a great leader and organizer should arise and form a union of these three forces and succeed in getting them to work in harmony, wars could be permanently eliminated and men could be taught to submerge their individual interests for the good of the race, and all this could take place within the time of this writer.

If we ever have a *successful* League of Nations, it will have to be created by and through these three great forces or else it will not permanently endure nor will it serve the purpose for which the present proposed league was organized.

Never, in the history of these great forces, have they worked in harmony with each other in any understanding. Never have they organized themselves so there was complete harmony of purpose in the individual ranks of the three.

Yet, the individuals composing these three great forces represent the highest strata in human civilization!

A first class football player, who understands the value of teamwork and the necessity of organization, might become this great leader if he were a man who could get the confidence and the co-operation of the leaders of these three forces.

These three great forces are:

1) The churches of the world;
2) The schools, public and private;
3) The newspapers and magazines.

Unfortunately these three great forces are divided among themselves, so that there is neither unity of purpose nor of effort in their ranks.

The churches are divided among themselves, but not hopelessly so. There is no doubt that all of the churches of the world could agree on concerted action in furthering a great movement which would supplement the work of each, and at the same time lay the foundation for a higher civilization.

The same can be said of the newspapers and magazines. Newspaper men have always given freely and willingly to the support of every movement that was for the benefit of the masses.

The public and private schools, through their directions constitute the most important factor in this trio of great powers, *because educators understand the principle which we are about to mention, and, for the further reason that any ideal can best be planted in the minds of the young during the early school period.*

Any ideal could be so permanently planted in the minds of children, through the joint efforts of these three great powers, that it would be impossible to erase it except through the manner in which it was planted.

A human being is the product of two causes. One is physical heredity and the other is environment, or mental heredity.

Every ambitious workman on earth is, potentially, an employer, because he is looking forward and planning the day when he can start a little business of his own.

Take the child of an uncivilized person, soon after birth, remove it from its parents and place it in a modern home, under the influence of a cultured environment, and that child will absorb most of the tendencies of the children in that home with whom it is raised. That which it inherited through physical heredity will remain with it forever, but from the moment of birth on it will take on the tendencies and the nature of those *with whom it closely associates.*

Ninety-nine per cent of the people of the world hold certain views of religion, politics, economics, and the like, because those views *were inherited from their parents or those with whom they were most closely associated before they reached the age of twelve years!*

Think it over!

You do not have to go outside of your own experience to prove the truth of this statement.

This being true, can you not see the importance of selecting with care that which is permitted to reach and influence the child mind before the age of twelve?

Can you not also see how any *ideal could be forced on the mind of the child, through systematic efforts upon parts of its early trainers, thus molding its mind after the ideal?*

Here in America a great problem has arisen to plague us. We have become the melting pot of the world. The people of every nationality, of every creed and of every temperament have flocked to our shores. These people have minds that are molded and set. Their viewpoints do not harmonize. The man and woman who was raised in Southern Italy have but little in common with those who were raised in America. When they come together they find themselves incompatible.

This great melting pot—this land of "milk and honey"—has attracted from other countries that class of people who come from the lowest strata, for the most part, the class which usually wants as much as it can get and is willing to give no more in return than it is compelled to give. A class which lacks culture and refinement.

There is not much that we can do to quiet the spirit of unrest among these adults, *but we can assimilate their offspring by forcing the American ideal on them* in our schools, churches and through our newspapers and magazines.

And what is our "American Ideal?"

Frankly, I do not know! I know what it used to be, a little over a hundred years ago, but interest in that particular ideal has waned considerably. The original American ideal has "run out," due to our neglect or our lack of understanding of the principle of "social heredity," the only source through which any ideal can be kept alive and passed on from one generation to another.

Some things we have kept alive, through this principle of social heredity, which we might well have allowed to fall by the wayside. For one thing we might have profitably allowed our spirit of "intolerance" to die with generations which have passed, but it is still with us; with us, because there has been no tendency to pass its opposite on to our offspring, through social heredity.

Instead of the old American ideal of which Washington, Jefferson, Paine, Franklin and Lincoln were examples, a new ideal has developed within the past fifty years. This new ideal is the mad desire for money! This desire has been passed from one generation to another, through social heredity, the offspring trying to emulate the parents in their rush to gain wealth. Men now look forward to becoming millionaires instead of great statesmen; they devote their efforts to personal gain instead of working for the good of the race, as did the prominent men a few generations back. We strive to emulate Rockefeller and Carnegie instead of Washington and Lincoln.

It may be best not to condemn that which you have not investigated, because this habit is an indication of a mind that is ruled by ignorance and prejudice.

This writer rises to remark that we need a few Washingtons and Lincolns along about now!

To whom may we turn in our search for unselfish leaders who are willing to submerge their own personal interests for the good of the race?

In the approaching race for the Presidency of the United States we see some eight or ten aspirants for the office, and *not a single man among them* is above suspicion, from one quarter or another, that his desire for the Presidency is *to gain more power instead of the unselfish one of rendering service for the good of the nation's masses.* Not a single piece of material which even remotely resembles Washington or Lincoln has been offered as a Presidential possibility.

But this is getting away from our main issue. That this lack of material exists all of us will agree. The important thing is, "How can we develop the right sort of material?" and the answer is, *"Through the principle of social heredity!"*

Through the combined efforts of the churches, schools and newspapers we could grow a superabundant crop of Washingtons, Lincolns and Jeffersons within a *single generation!*

Not only could we do this, but we could change the whole thinking process of the world, replacing the desire to *get* with the higher desire of *giving;* the common tendency to tear down with the nobler one of building up; the selfish desire for personal aggrandizement with the higher one of submerging personal interests for the good of the race.

The time has come for a *round-table meeting of all the churches of the world, all the newspaper and magazine publishers, and all of the educators!*

When these three forces reach out across the distance separating the continents and begin to work in unity, with harmony of purpose, *the world during the next few generations can be made to resemble whatever they wish it to resemble.*

Meanwhile, there is much good that these powers can do for the adults of the world, through the use of the right sort of propaganda.

The leaders of the German empire have shown the world what can be accomplished, *in a single generation,* through application of the principle of *social heredity!*

Let us not so soon forget this lesson!

We defeated the Germans on the battlefields of Europe, but the price we paid in order to do this was in vain unless we follow this defeat with a greater victory here at home, through the *power of social heredity!*

It lies within the power of the churches, schools, and newspapers to control the world by establishing a new and higher ideal in the minds of the individuals, through the principle of social heredity. If these three great leaders do not grasp this wonderful opportunity, the responsibility for our continued unhappy state will rest upon their shoulders.

If the churches, schools and newspapers would pool their efforts and systematically *force* the Golden Rule philosophy upon the minds of the next generation, wars, both between *nations* and *individuals,* could be eliminated!

The desire to *get* without *giving* could be wiped out!

The tendency to work for selfish, personal gain instead of submerging personal interests for the good of the race, could be wiped out.

The "hive spirit" could be permanently injected into the human mind!

There is plenty of everything in this world for all, but until the individual develops a passion for *helping* the weaker of the race instead of *exploiting* him, a few will continue to have more than they need or can use, while the majority will remain in poverty and want!

No law, no voting power on earth, can change this! The change can only come through operation of the principle of social heredity.

There are some bees in every hive which would starve to death if it were not for the hive spirit, in which the individual works for the good of the hive. In fact, every bee in the hive would starve to death during the winter if it were not for the hive spirit through which the honey is pooled for the good of all.

When I see men trying to solve these great economic problems by disputations, argument, organization of physical force, political parties and the like, I think of the little dog which runs along and barks at a passing train, foolishly imagining that it can stop the train.

The very men who are clamoring for the upper hand in the industrial world today, railing and cursing the present leaders of industry, would find themselves in the receiver's court in a few weeks if the industries of this country were turned over to them, *because they lack leaders who are sound in economics, and, for the more important reason that they would be unwilling to submerge their individual interests for the good of the whole, thus leading to disagreement among themselves.*

Who will be the first to step out of the ranks and become a great organizer and leader, using the principle of social heredity as his coworker?

The man who does this, if he be a real leader, will do more for posterity than any man of the past whose record history records.

Study carefully for the hidden motive which actuates the man who tries to fasten his leadership on you without your consent.

And, may it not be possible that we need a few more men and women who are unselfish enough, and whose vision is broad enough, to make it their business to sow a crop of wholesome seed for the future generations?

Our ideas, like our forests, are rapidly being dissipated and depleted. The field in which they can be re-sown is the human mind, and the process through which this sowing can be done is social heredity, which means—ideals which we plant in the plastic minds of our young! One generation of this systematic use of the principle of social (or mental) heredity will raise our ideals as high as we aspire to raise them! If Germany forced "kultur" on her young through the churches, schools and newspapers, in a single generation, we can force the Golden Rule on ours in the same length of time, because the principle is effective and easily applied. Every educator, every first class newspaper editor and every church leader understands this power which we refer to as social heredity, but there will be no quick results until all of these work in unity, in an organized manner.

Perhaps the Interchurch World movement offers the

nucleus for an organization of these three great forces. If so, and the right sort of a leader is available, this movement can easily become the most far-reaching of any in life history of the world.

The thing about which I am writing seems to be a gigantic undertaking, but it can be completed at less than the amount which the Panama Canal cost, within about the same length of time.

Let me repeat my statement so it will not be forgotten: The churches, schools and newspapers could, within *one single generation,* so thoroughly establish a new ideal in the minds of the world that men would turn their efforts toward helping the weaker of the race; they would do this just as naturally as they now exploit the weaker of the race. This could be brought about through the principle of social heredity–planting an ideal in the minds of the young!

I am tempted to say that the schools, alone, could successfully do this work. I am sure the schools and churches, combined, could perform the task, although it could be done in less time through the aid of organized propaganda through the newspapers and magazines.

Control that which the child is taught in school, that which is taught in the church, and that which is published in the public press, and you may be sure that the power which does this controlling will have, in a single generation, the exact sort of an ideal it desires.

Funny little men run about here and there, preaching this, that and the other panacea for the world's evils, few of them having the remotest sort of idea how to put into operation that which they offer as a remedy.

They remind one of so many geese, chattering and flopping their wings just before feeding time, grumbling because the keeper is late with the feed, but having not the slightest idea how to hurry him along.

In all this talk about a League of Nations; in all this talk about the downtrodden working class, not one single intelligent solution has been offered, because those who had formulas foolishly expected to apply them to and through the adult mind, in a few month's time.

I suspect the world's evils did not arise overnight, but, to the contrary, they have arisen out of ages and ages of misdirected efforts, through a blind application of this principle of social heredity.

If you MUST slander those whom you do not like, be careful not to speak your grievance, but write it—write it in the sands, near the water's edge.

I suspect that if some bright, far-sighted chap had started a movement about two or three generations ago, with the object of supplementing the work of the churches, schools and newspaper with a practical application of the Golden Rule, as it applies to the world of economics, the history of the world would be different today.

This could have been done, just as it can now be done, through the principle of social heredity.

The man who offers a remedy for the world's evils and expects it to become operative through any other principle, knows nothing of the nature of the human mind!

You can tame a wildcat by taking the young animal away from its mother's breast before she has had time to instill in its mind, through this same principle of social heredity, fear of and antagonism toward man, but not afterward. The same principle applies to the higher animal, man! If man ever learns how to be decent to his fellow men, he will learn it because of an ideal that was forced on his mind before he reaches the age of twelve—make no mistake about this.

All the preaching in the world will not change this. Man no longer fears fire and brimstone in the next world, therefore, if he treats the weaker of his race with kindness and extends them the helping hand he will do so because he wills to do so, and he is not apt to will to do so unless this desire is planted in his mind, as an ideal, while his mind is plastic.

The human mind is the only great mystery in the world which should interest human beings, because the human mind, when properly directed, can transform the most common sort of person into a genius!

If you understand even the elementary principles of psychology you know exactly what is meant by the term social (or mental) heredity; also, you understand the soundness of the suggestions, concerning the possibilities available to the world, through the organized efforts of the churches, schools and newspapers. If you have never given much study to psychology, get some good books (those that are written in simple, laymen's language) on this subject and inform yourself. To familiarize yourself with the principles of the human mind is to understand the only real power on this earth that can help you get to wherever you are going in life.

If this editorial should cause you to take an interest in the study of psychology and result in your reading upon the subject and thinking about it as you read, it no doubt will mean an important turning point in your life.

To save you the trouble of looking up a good book on psychology, I am going to quote the following, by Arthur Brisbane, which appeared in the Chicago Herald-Examiner:

"This is about *your* brain.

"A rich boy inherits an automobile, orders the chauffeur to bring it around, takes little interest in the machinery.

"A man who has worked for the money to buy an automobile tries to know about it–it interests him.

"We inherit our brains, get them ready-made at birth. Few know more about the wonderful thinking machine at the end of life than at the beginning.

"Whatever of you amounts to anything is the mysterious power working through the brain. What actually does the work, *Soul,* as some tell you, *Will,* as others say, *Chemical Reaction,* as materialists believe, we cannot know. But we can know about the machine that lives in the dark inside the skull, receiving information of the outside world through one set of nerves and through another set issuing orders obeyed by muscles and bones.

"Read, among many good books on the subject, 'Brain and Personality,' by W.H. Thompson, who understands his subject. It is published by Dodd, Mead & Co.

"Men, originally, did not know that feeling and thinking dwell in the brain. The word 'brain' doesn't occur in the Bible. When the book was written it wasn't suspected that the cold, gray organ isolated in the skull had anything to do with thought.

"Babylonians, and others later, believed that thought was in the liver. Their priests carefully examined, for information about the future, livers of animals offered in sacrifice.

"The Jews believed that the soul was located in the heart, the mind in the kidneys, the gentle emotions, compassion, etc., in the bowels. Therefore, the Bible says 'his reins (kidneys) instruct him in the night seasons.' Elsewhere it is said 'The Lord trieth the heart and the kidneys,' and Jeremiah denounced the hypocrites who, he said, 'had the Lord in their mouths, but not in their kidneys.'

"Aristotle decided that the brain had nothing to do with thought, that it was a refrigerating plant to cool off the blood.

"One man, Alcmaeon, who lived before Plato or Aristotle, taught that the mind was in the brain. He based his belief on discovery that total blindness was caused if you cut the optic nerve leading from the eyes to the brain. Otherwise men scouted the theory until the great Greek Galen, physician to Marcus Aurelius, revived and proved it.

"Broca, scientist, who died in 1881, was first to understand the human thinking machine. The part of your brain with which you speak is called 'Broca's convolution.' He located speech in the rear part of the third frontal convolution; injury to that part destroys speech absolutely. When that Frenchman successfully explored the brain and taught how it worked, he did more important exploring than a thousand Pearys,

Livingstones or Stanleys.

"As you possess two eyes, two ears, two hands and two feet, so you possess *two brains.* Each brain is complete, separate, and can, if necessary, do all the work of thinking, just as one eye, if necessary, can do the work of seeing.

Money and happiness, the two great objects of life never have been attained and RETAINED, except through rendering useful service.

"If you are right-handed, the convolution in your *left* brain does the talking. If you are left-handed, it is the *right-handed* convolution that talks. If the talking part of the brain is destroyed in a young child, the other brain can be taught to talk. In a man of fifty, injury to 'Broca's convolution' destroys speech for life. The brain becomes hardened with age and, like an old dog, cannot be taught new tricks.

"We are born with no knowledge of speech. Each new brain must be taught everything from the beginning, speech included. Education begins when a baby points its hand and is told the name of the thing to which it points. If you tied the left hand of a child, compelling it to point only with its right, speech would surely begin with the left brain. If you tied down the right hand and compelled the child to point with its left, it would be left-handed and the right brain alone would learn to speak.

"Seeing, hearing, recognizing our friends, tasting, smelling, everything that we do, has its separate place in the brain, as a book has its place on the library shelf. Your brain can be so damaged as to make it impossible for you to recognize members of your own family, although you would see them. Injury in another place would destroy sight. One injury would make it impossible for you to tell one sound for another, the bark of a dog from the song of a bird. You would hear noises, but not know their meaning. Another brain injury would make you deaf for life. As the left-handed man speaks with the right side of the brain, and vice versa, so the man left-handed hears and understands sound only with the right side of the brain.

"Nobody knows *how* the mind works or what the thought is that enables a two-legged animal, glued to this earth, to measure accurately the distance of a fixed star, billions of miles away, weigh the sun, or announce with accuracy the weight of this earth.

"One theory teaches that the mind is like an aeolian harp, giving out thought when outside forces strike it, as the aeolian harp makes music when struck by the wind. The other important theory likens the brain to a violin, that, no matter how skillfully made, must be played upon by thinking being, before it can produce music.

"*What* works the brain, or *how* or *why,* no one knows. The ancients said the earth rested on the shoulders of the giant Atlas. Atlas stood on the turtle, and there they let it drop. It didn't seem worthwhile to ask upon what the turtle stood.

"We say that our nerves of sight, smell, taste, touch and hearing inform the brain. The brain informs the consciousness, the consciousness orders the will, and the will gives orders to the body. The will, like the thing that the turtle stood on, remains unexplained.

"When you put on another man's hat and it falls over your ears, you are indignant. You know the other man concludes that he is your mental superior. That does not follow.

You can no more reap a generous crop of pay from a sowing of a poor grade of service than you could reap a crop of wheat from a sowing of wild mustard.

"A brain of normal size is usually better than the brain abnormally small. Idiots and half-witted persons usually have small heads, and lighter brains than normal human beings.

"Helmholtz, one of the world's most learned men, had a brain weighing only forty-five ounces. Thirteen men that died in an English poorhouse had brains weighing more than sixty ounces. Webster's brain weighed only a little over fifty-five ounces.

"Dollinger, learned student and expounder of theology, had a brain weighing thirty-seven ounces.

"Among five races, Swedish, Bavarian, Hessian, Bohemian and English, the English are found to have the smallest average brain weight, the Bohemian the highest.

"Size of head and weight of brain do not always go together. A brain, like an orange, may have a thick covering.

"A small saw, of the right kind of steel, will cut through a big iron bar. A small brain, of the right material, is more important than mere brain bulk.

"Women's brains, as well as their skulls, are smaller than men's, on the average.

"As time passes, the substance of which your brain is made 'sets,' becomes, mentally speaking, hard, like concrete. After a certain age a man cannot change his opinions. He thinks he doesn't *want* to, but in reality he cannot.

"Between twenty and thirty and forty educated men receive new ideas easily, after that with difficulty or not at all. Unless an opening has been made into the brain, through which the truth may go, in youth, the truth cannot get in later. Hence the importance of having what is contemptuously called 'a smattering of general information and general opinions.' Each 'smatter' may leave a hole to let in the light later. Uneducated men rarely accept a new thought after 25. Beyond that age they can hate, but think with difficulty. That makes mobs so dangerous.

"When Harvey announced that the blood circulates through the body, pumped by the heart, any fool, you would say, should immediately have recognized the truth of Harvey's discovery.

"Yet that truth, so plain to us, was denied by all the 'great doctors' of Europe, except some of those under 40 years of age. The minds of the others had settled into solid concrete.

"Voltaire in his chapter on 'Statesmen' in the 'Philosophical Dictionary' says he does not write for statesmen of his day, because they haven't time to listen, but for the young men that will be statesmen later. You cannot model or reform solid concrete.

"The scientific world is puzzled by the fact that we should have two complete brains, as we have two feet and two hands. The second brain seems unnecessary; still we all have it, ready, in case of accident to the speaking brain, to take up the work of speech, thought and perception, if the accident comes early enough.

"Nature does her big work in spherical form. The sums and planets are spheres, water in the brook or the blood in your veins rolls in round drops. Perhaps there is a good reason, to be developed later, for a spherical brain with its two hemispheres. Some day we may use one brain for our little work of thought and organization on this earth, the other for exploration and contemplation of the outside universe. 'It hath not yet been shown what we shall be.'

Why not pay the incompetent, lazy, unskilled workman the same wages as the man who is skilled, industrious and highly efficient? Would you if you were the employer?

"The two brains that live back of your eyes, above your nose and ears and under your hair, deepening their convolutions, increasing their power as long as you think, deteriorating with dreadful rapidity when you stop thinking, are separated by a cleft and united, at the bottom of the cleft, by an interesting bridge called *corpus callosum.* It is a bridge of white fibres passing from one brain to the other. Information is supposed to travel over this bridge from one brain to the other. There is no certainty as to its use. Men have lived normally without it.

"Someday, the experiment of transplanting one-half of a very young human brain in the place of one-half of the brain of a young chimpanzee may be attempted. Anti-vivisectionists, take warning.

"Like yourself, your little brother, the chimpanzee, has two complete brains. And you would find it difficult to tell the brain of the chimpanzee child from that of a human child.

"Your brain has its bark like that of a tree, called the 'cortex,' and below that a white, cold substance, like the hard wood inside of a tree. The thinking is all done in the brain bark or cortex; thought apparently flows in there, as the life-giving sap flows in the tree's bark.

"As all your seeing, hearing and identifying is done in one of your brains, so all of your thinking is done in one brain, never in both at once. An accident of childhood can decide which shall be the working brain and which the idle brain, through life.

"It was a great shock to the superficial when it was shown that the chimpanzee's brain possesses not only every lobe, but every convolution of the human brain. 'Broca's convolution' is there, only the monkey cannot speak.

"Huxley even proved, against Owen, that there is not in the human brain one single peculiarity missing from the low brain of a baboon. The dissecting knife cannot explain the difference that separates, in worth, the baboon's brain from the brain of a scientist.

"No animal talks or ever has said a word, with all respect to the late Dr. Garner. No human race has ever been known that did not possess speech, however low its intelligence. Every word you say to express all your thought is located 'in a small part of gray matter not larger than a hazel nut.' Break a blood vessel in that part of your brain and you are dumb.

"Injure that part of the brain slightly, and you may forget how to speak English, yet be able to retain your knowledge of French or of some dead language. The mental 'shelf' holding the English language may be destroyed, and the French or Greek 'shelf' remain intact.

" 'I think, therefore I am,' the scientist says. *Why* we think or *how* we think or what it is that thinks, whether thought is real, created by us, or printed on our minds from the outside, as the sun's light prints a photograph on a plate, we do not know.

"Even sleep, the brain's vacation, is a dark mystery to us.

What happens when the brain sleeps and the body rests? Does mind, spirit, consciousness, or whatever the thinking machine is, go off to enjoy itself elsewhere, as the chauffeur leaves his car when he runs it into the garage for the night?

"You must say, 'We sleep because we are tired.' Part of us is tried, part is not. Everything that requires effort of the *will* causes fatigue. If your will makes you work, run or jump, you tire and must rest. But one part of your brain working unconsciously puts upon certain nerves or muscles a task that lasts, without ceasing, for a hundred years, if you live as long, without a second's interruption, night or day.

"The power that you use in taking a single breath, using the muscles of the chest and abdomen, is equal to the strength that would be required to raise five hundred pounds one inch. More than thirty times every minute, as long as you live, certain muscles act with power enough to lift five hundred pounds one inch from the floor, and they never rest.

"And that wonderful engine and muscle, the heart, how does it last without rest? Carrel, the French surgeon, operating on the lung cavity of a dog, held in his hand, without injuring it, the animal's beating heart, saying, 'the most wonderful engine in the world.' It is that, in animals and in us. Something in your brain of which you know nothing, keeps the heart working.

"Two nerves, running from the lower part of your brain, the 'medulla,' to the heart, regulate the work of that engine. Stimulate one of those nerves with an electric current, your heart instantly doubles, its speed and power. Stimulate the other nerve, the heart beats more slowly. Over-stimulate it and the heart stops. Cut that second nerve running to the heart, and the heart races like a team of horses with the reins cut.

"One nerve drives the heart faster, like the whip in the coachman's hand; another one holds it back, like the reins fastened to the bridle. And, as the heart's action is controlled, so everything within our bodies, 'fearfully and wonderfully made,' is controlled, from the brain's dark cortex, muscles and nerves, that regulate blood pressure, marvelous system that controls the body's heat so that blood temperature doesn't change a fraction of a degree between the equator and the North Pole. And about all that automatic management, we feel and know nothing.

"Who ever reads a book on anatomy, or psychology, asks at the end, 'What is the thing about which I have been reading? What is it that lives within us, recognizing facts reported by the nerves, sending out through the feeble hands and words of man orders that change the earth's surface, tear down mountains and unite oceans?'

Ask me a question which I will find hard to answer and you will have rendered me a genuinely useful service by causing me to THINK!

"Two thousand four hundred years ago, Democritus, of Abdera, taught by the Chaldean Magi, said, 'Man lives plunged in a world of illusion and of deceptive forms which the vulgar take for reality. To tell the truth, we do not know anything.'

"Learned physicians and physiologists of today study 'tissue,' nerves, muscles and also confess, concerning the power ruling us, that we 'do not know anything.' Only the flash of the eye reveals the indweller,' the soul. But does it? The horse's eye seems to flash, as he neighs and paws the ground, hearing the bugle blow. Has he also an indweller of a lower grade?"

You have just read a very fine and a very easily understood lesson on psychology. If you thought and digested that which you read you now know more about psychology—the human mind—than ninety-nine percent of the people of the world know about it. You understand, now, why I recommend organized effort upon the part of the churches, schools and newspapers in planting the Golden Rule Philosophy in the minds of the young, *because this is the only place where it can be made to stick!*

After you finish reading this, go to your public library and read, "The Science of Power," by Benjamin Kidd (published by G. P. Putnam's Sons, New York). Also, "Thinking as a Science," by Henry Hazlitt (published by E. P. Dutton & Company, New York). Either of these books can be supplied by your local book store, or by Montgomery Ward & Company, Chicago, Illinois.

After you read these two interesting books–which will require not more than a few hours–you will know more about the human mind than all the people of the world, except that relatively small number who have specialized in psychology. Incidentally, you will possess all the way from ten to ten thousand times as much power to attain your chief aim in life as you possessed before doing this prescribed reading *and thinking!*

The difference between the $25,000.00-a-year-man and the $1,500.00-a-year-man is largely a difference of understanding of the principles of psychology. Inform yourself on this subject and see that those in whom you are interested are likewise informed.

You now have the idea!

What are you going to do with it? When? How? If this editorial has caused an idea to shape itself in your mind, be sure to keep that idea alive and at work! Tell others about it–write about it–think about it, because all this is mental exercise which will develop the idea more and more until it becomes a part of you, and then you will use it as freely and as skillfully as you use your right hand, but it will help you produce that which a million right hands could never produce without it.

It will teach you to think accurately and reason logically. It will carry you into leadership that will not end until you get to be the person whom you wish to be!

My definite aim in life is:

To place principle above the dollar and humanity above the selfish individual who would get without giving, and to help my fellowmen do the same.

To sow the seeds of revolution in the hearts of my

fellowmen until they rise and work with co-ordinated effort to the common end that civilization may offer something greater than the privilege of being bound to the weary treadmill of toil, and of standing, always, in fear of starvation.

To master intolerance and help others do the same.

To carry on a constructive educational program that will help men and women see the advantages of co-operation and the disadvantages of fighting one another in their mad scramble to worship at the shrine of mammon.

To organize a chain of newspapers that will spread, like a net, over America, and whose pages will carry only clean, constructive, truthful news, and whose editorials will arouse and inspire millions of people until they free themselves from the eternal grind of the wage bound and get out from under the heels of the mad money getters.

To render service that is greater in quality and quantity than is paid for, and to help others see the advantages of doing likewise.

To lay aside prejudice and lend a helping hand to all, regardless of their religious, political, racial or economic tendencies.

To scatter seeds of sunshine wherever I go, aiming, always, to create a welcome for my presence.

To remember that I am a public servant, and that the greatest honor which can come to a man is the honor of serving well!

To gain the confidence of my fellowmen by first deserving it, and, to so conduct myself that this confidence will never be undermined or betrayed.

Finally, to accept whatever responsibilities life may bring, seeking always to serve and never to shirk; always to help and never to hinder the wheels of progress as they roll on toward that goal for which every human being is striving–*Happiness Here on Earth.*

BILLBOARD 15

APPLYING THE GOLDEN RULE

The fifteenth billboard on the road to success is *applying the Golden Rule.*

And now comes a professor in Harvard University with a letter that starts our editorial typewriter to clicking. We print both the letter and our reply, with the object of giving our readers a chance to do some thinking on the subject under discussion.

> "My dear Mr. Hill:
>
> "I have been a reader of your magazine ever since the first edition appeared four years ago, and I have studied your philosophy with sustained and increasing interest from month to month.
>
> "It has been very illuminating to watch the development of your own reasoning process since you began writing these uplift essays, and I have reason to believe that you have accomplished more good than you are aware of; however, I have been disappointed because you do not seem to have yet discovered that the Golden Rule, within itself, is not sufficient to carry a man to success.
>
> "Think it over and it will be very obvious to you that a man could easily starve to death in the midst of plenty and still apply the Golden Rule in all of his transactions with others.
>
> "Pardon this intrusion, but I know from your

> literary works that you are a man who welcomes suggestions, even though they do not harmonize with your own viewpoint.
>
> Very cordially,"

The foregoing letter came as a mild shock to us. Is it possible that a professor of Harvard has been reading after us for four years without correctly interpreting that which we wrote? Undoubtedly so, and we take the blame to ourself. That is, we take the blame up to the present point, but from here on we pass the buck by frankly saying that if the Harvard professor or anyone else who reads these lines fails to understand our viewpoint regarding the relationship of the Golden Rule to success, it will not be our fault for we are going to be plain.

To begin with, we disclaim having ever stated that the Golden Rule, alone, is sufficient to carry any one to success, because we have known for many years that it is not. According to our viewpoint there are many factors that enter into success, not the least important of which is the definition of the word success, itself.

Let us say, for the sake of illustration, that the accumulation of money in excess of actual requirements for living, is success.

Money is accumulated through the application of power; mind you, I said "accumulated," which is not the same as "inherited."

Power comes through organized effort; in no other way. When you develop power through organized effort you bring together many factors and blend them, in the right proportion; then you put the result of this blending of factors back of a well-organized plan. This plan varies according to the nature of the station in life or the thing you aim to acquire through its use.

There are fifteen of these factors out of which power may be developed, and we have mentioned them in these columns scores of times, from every angle and viewpoint that we could conceive, because we knew that this was necessary in order to make our premise clear to people of varying ability to interpret.

It can do no harm if we mention these fifteen factors once more; nor will it do any harm if we repeat that power may be developed from a proper blending of these fifteen factors.

The first one is a *definite* aim in life!

Then follow the other fourteen, namely, Self-Confidence, Initiative, Imagination, Action, Enthusiasm, Self-Control, The Habit of Performing More Work than Paid For, An Attractive Personality, Accurate Thought, Concentration, Persistence, Learning from Failures and Mistakes, Tolerance and last, but by no means least, applying the Golden Rule.

We have never said that the Golden Rule, alone, was sufficient. It comes at the end of the list, but we say now, that which we have said many times before, in scores of different ways, that *no position in life can endure and no success can be permanent unless based upon truth and justice,* which is the same as saying, that success will not last unless it was attained through the application of the Golden Rule principle.

Wealth is in the hands of those who have the intelligence with which to get it and hold it. There is no escape from this fact.

The law of the survival of the fittest prevails, and always will. Any student of Darwin knows that there is such a law and knows, also, how it works. Nature creates enormous numbers of field mice, the majority of which find their way into the stomach of the hawk, the owl, the weasel or some other more "fit" creature. The word "fit" is not the same as the word "just." Perhaps the field mice that feed the owl are as "just" as those that escape and propagate the species, but they are not as "fit," meaning that they are not organized and have not sufficient power to survive.

In every specie of animal, including the human race, there are certain individuals that are favored with superior "fitness" to survive.

Never in the history of the world has there been such abundant opportunity as there is now for the person who is willing to serve before trying to collect.

The man who knows how to organize his efforts and intelligently direct them can get all the money his imagination can conceive, and there is nothing on this earth that can stop him. Whether he will be happy and "successful" with it after he gets it is a different matter. Success, as we understand it, must include happiness, but there is no doubt that men can get money in large quantities without applying the Golden Rule or enjoying happiness over the possession of the money after they get it.

The fifteen factors herein mentioned contemplate the use of organized effort, or power, in a way that will bring *real success:* the sort that is well mixed with happiness.

Most men have at least a portion of these fifteen factors already under their control, but what they need is the addition of those which they have not built into their scheme of life. One could have the first fourteen factors well under control, but, if he failed to guide his efforts by the fifteenth he could not be a permanent success. Power could be developed by a proper blending of the first fourteen factors, but that power might lead to destruction instead of success, if it were not guided by the Golden Rule principle.

If this does not make clear our viewpoint with reference to the relationship of the Golden Rule to success we must plead inability to express our meaning through the English language.

Most of the great achievements have been born of struggle!

Nature has arranged her plans so that every living thing must progress through struggle. This necessary struggle is often very disagreeable, and most of us would shield ourselves from it if we knew how.

The greater our struggle the more we learn.

Nature plants desires in our hearts and then surrounds the object of these desires with many obstacles that we must overcome before we attain the thing desired. Nowhere do we find it a part of Nature's plans to hand us something for nothing. She makes us strive for everything we get, and she makes us pay a price for it.

One of the most deeply seated desires of the human heart is that of possession of wealth.

The man who is not urged into action by this desire for wealth is an oddity among his fellowmen. Inasmuch as this desire is so universal we have reason to believe that Nature placed it in the human heart as a means of causing us to struggle.

Whether we get all that we struggle for in this world or not we ought to take comfort from the thought that we have at least had the privilege of struggling, and that out of this struggle we have learned something that may serve Nature's plans further along the way.

The moment we stop struggling we begin to atrophy and finally die. Nature says "you must keep growing or get out of the way." We cannot grow without struggle. This ought to give us comfort when the struggle seems hardest, because rapid growth comes from hard struggle.

When you lose your sense of humor get a job on an elevator for your life will be a series of *ups* and *downs*.

Fear is a terrible drawback. Among the most dangerous and repressive fears is that of what other people will say about us. Bald-headed men could save their hair if they were not afraid to leave off the hats, with the tight bands that cut off the nerve lines that feed the roots of the hair. But, fear of "what they will say" keeps men from leaving off their hats.

We recently asked a public man what he thought to be the real cause of so many strikes. He told us, but before he did so he pledged us to a promise not to mention his name. He, too, was afraid of what "they would say" about him for expressing his honest opinion about the labor situation.

That indefinite, imaginary "they" has kept many a genius imprisoned in his own head because of fear to act and express himself frankly.

Suppose people do criticize you? What of it? Any fool can

criticize, and *a lot of them do!* But their criticism doesn't hurt anyone except themselves. It marks them for what they are.

Men who analyze and think seldom criticize themselves with frankness. The man or woman who boldly does what seems to be right, even though it may not be in conformity with the views of the crowd, possesses strength of character that knows no such words as "I fear," and "impossible."

I have just talked with one of these thinkers. He did not pledge me to omit his name. When I asked him what he thought about the present labor situation he quickly replied: "If labor should win all it asks for, which it will not, we might as well move to Russia, where they make no pretense of permitting the people to enjoy freedom. The present issue between capital and labor is clear and easily defined. Capital is fighting for the right of men to work where they please, for whomsoever they please, and under whatever arrangement they please. Labor is fighting to exclude from employment all who do not pay tribute to the self-imposed leaders of labor. If labor should win it would mean that the very fundamental principle upon which the Declaration of Independence was founded would be swept aside and we would no longer have ground to boast of this being the freest country in the world."

Anything nebulous about that statement?

Whether we agree with it or not we have the highest respect for the man who had the courage to thus frankly express himself.

Right is right, and wrong is wrong, and the man who is afraid to call each by its proper name is not entitled to the benefits of that which is right nor immunity from the effects of that which is wrong.

Whether we agree with him or not we have every respect for the man who stands on his two legs, looks the world squarely in the face without flinching and tells it what he believes.

In front of the typewriter on which these lines are being written hangs a big sign that reads as follows: *"I am becoming more successful every day in every way!"*

A "hard-boiled egg" who is a friend of ours was admitted into the royal sanctorum for a few minutes and as soon as his eye lit on this sign he said: "You don't believe that stuff, do you?" and I replied: "Of course not! All it ever did for me was to help me get out of the coal mines and find a place in the world where I am serving upwards of 100,000 people in whose minds I am planting the same positive thought that this sign brings out, therefore, why should I believe in it?"

As he started to leave he said: "Well, perhaps there is something to this sort of philosophy after all. I have always feared that I would be a failure all my life and so far my fears have been thoroughly realized."

You are condemning yourself to poverty, misery and failure, or, you are driving yourself on toward the heights of attainment, solely *by the thoughts you think.* If you *demand* success of yourself and back your demands up with plenty of action you are bound to find success. There is a difference between *demanding* success and just merely wishing for it. You must find out what this difference is and take advantage of it.

If you do not feel as bold as does this writer you might try this experiment on yourself for a couple of weeks: Every leisure moment you have say to yourself–"*I am becoming more successful every day in every way."*

Write the same words out on a card and carry this where you can read it several times a day. When you say these words over to yourself say them with positive assurance that they will be realized. Keep this up with persistence, but do not go about it with a half way feeling that it is some "foolish experiment" that might get results but probably will not.

Do you remember what the Bible says (somewhere in the book of Matthew) about those who have the faith as a grain of mustard seed? Go at this with at least that much faith; more if you can do so.

Never mind about what "they will say" or what "they will think" about you, because "they" will know nothing about your experiment. If you will go at this plan with persistence born of faith you will soon become so powerful and so able to solve your own problems that you will not care what "they say."

If you have only a hundred dollars left invest it in a new suit and look prosperous. Like attracts like.

Oh ye weak-kneed of little faith! Get wise to yourselves and claim your own. You have within that "mind stuff" that reposes in your head, all the power you need to get everything you need, and about the simplest way of telling you how to use this power is to tell you to *believe in yourself.*

This writer knows a man of fifty who is one of the most versatile men of his acquaintance. This man knows world history from the beginning to the present. He is of strong physique and makes an impressive appearance. He has a wonderful, rhythmic voice that plays with perfect harmony upon the ears of all who hear it. He has an attractive personality. People like him and trust him. He has thousands of friends throughout America. Best of all, he has good health and at least forty active years ahead of him yet. With all these advantages the poor "simp" is getting nowhere because—

—Because he does not know the power he possesses!

There would be some excuse for him if he were not an able philosopher and did not understand how to reason from *cause* to *effect,* or from *effect* back to its *cause.* There is nothing within the gift of the American people that he could not have if he had the self-confidence to *demand* more of himself.

Be it remembered that the real way to get the co-operation of others is to *demand* much from yourself!

The man of whom we write resembles a horse that has been bridled, saddled and harnessed by a man with less than one-tenth of its physical power. If the horse ever did any thinking and saw that it had all this physical power no man would ever harness it again. Ditto with the man of whom we write. He has the power, not physical alone, but the power of all powers—the mental, but he doesn't know that he has it, consequently he is doing the slow goose-step down the dusty road to failure and decay.

"Know thyself, man! Know thyself."

This has been the cry of the philosophers for ages. When you know yourself you will know that there is nothing foolish about hanging a sign in front of your daily work that reads:

"I am becoming more successful every day in every way."

Until you do know yourself such a sign would indicate nothing except that the man using it was an eccentric person.

If you are averse to experimenting on yourself here is one that you can try out on some other person: Pick out some person who has but little ambition; one of the mediocre type, and begin to shower that person with suggestions that he seems to be doing better work; that he seems to be growing more ambitious; that he seems more self-reliant. Prophesy a great career for him. Keep this up as often as you come in contact with this person and watch what happens. Very soon your suggestions will begin to get into his sub-conscious mind; he will begin to spur himself up and before he realizes it your suggestion will have been transformed by him into auto-suggestion, or self-suggestion and he will live the part and become the person that you pictured in his mind.

It sometimes happens that an idle remark, dropped in a fertile mind that is ready to receive it, at the right time, will change the entire career of a person. We have such a case in mind. A friend of ours was engaged in the typewriter business. One day he was bragging about the fact that he knew personally every purchaser and every stenographer who operated the typewriters sold through his office. He really felt proud of his ability to know all these people. An ordinary young man stenographer was listening, and he asked this question:

"Aren't you limiting your possibilities by carrying all that useless detail in your head?"

This question made our friend angry, thanks for that! What right had an ordinary stenographer to ask him, a man of influence and success, such a question?

Out of this anger came a revelation!

He began to think the remark over and the more he thought about it the more he saw what the stenographer had in mind. Overnight he changed his policy and began to turn all details of his business over to subordinates. Today he is a wealthy man, retired from active business at the age of forty-two, with plenty of money in the bank and trustworthy managers who carry on his business and continue to turn money into the bank for him.

The most important turning-points in life usually come through some simple remark or happening that seems of little significance at the time.

Generally speaking, anything that brings us up with a bang and makes us check up our philosophy and reinforce it where it is weak, is good for us. The mind is quick to atrophy and become lazy and inactive if we take things easily and permit nothing to force the mind out of its ordinary daily routine way of functioning.

There may be short-cuts to success, but many a weary traveler gets stuck in the mud trying to go that way.

It often happens that a death in the family or some other shocking catastrophe serves to re-direct the course of one's mind and force it into new and more efficient channels. Nearly every failure serves as a mental tonic that can be made to and will tune up the entire mental apparatus if one will permit it to do so.

This writer has a few enemies, thank God for that! These enemies work for us day and night, although they do not know it. They work for us by keeping us on the alert lest we give them some opening through which to annihilate us or destroy our plans.

Do we hate our enemies?

No! We used to hate them, but that was before we discovered how valuable they were. Mind you, we do not love our enemies; haven't progressed that far yet, but we make no effort to discourage them or kill off their efforts, because that would be as foolish as would be the farmer if he killed off all the weeds on his farm, thus taking away the substance that fertilizes the soil and keeps it alive year after year.

The eleventh commandment says: "Select thy booze with care lest thy days on earth be cut short."

Every successful man must have a flock of enemies!

Show us a person who has no enemies and we will show you, at the same time, a person who lacks the self-confidence and the courage and the personality to stick his head above those of the "common herd" who drift with time and events.

Enemies are one of the most valuable assets of the person who looks upon them philosophically and understands the nature of the service they are unwittingly and unintentionally rendering him.

Is this not a consoling thought to all who have been worrying because not everyone likes them? It is your thought; appropriate it and make use of it. That's what we are passing it on for.

Last night we picked up Emerson's essays and read his essay on "Spiritual Laws."

A strange thing happened! We saw in that essay, which we had read scores of times before, many things we had never seen during the previous readings. With pencil in hand we read with heated enthusiasm, as though we had never read the essay before.

It was so strange that we stopped and analyzed the experience. We found that we had seen, during previous readings, all that *we were capable of interpreting at the time.* We saw more in the selfsame words this time because the unfoldment of our mind since the last reading had prepared us to interpret more.

The human mind is constantly unfolding, like the petals of a flower, until it reaches its maximum development. What this maximum is, where it ends, where it leads to, varies with the individual and the use that he gives his mind. A mind that is forced or coaxed into analytical thought every day seems to keep on unfolding and developing greater powers of interpretation, without limitation.

This writer is satisfied that no mind is developed to anywhere near its maximum before the age of fifty to sixty years. If this theory is sound, how foolish it is for one to begin to select a nice quiet burial place and get ready to die when he begins to reach the most useful period of life, fifty to sixty.

Last night the goddess of dreams stood beside our bed. She said, "Arise, mortal, and express a wish–just one–and it shall be granted instantly."

We hesitated; the dream angel spoke again. She said, "Is it money, power, fame, health, friends?" To which we replied:

"No, dream angel, it is none of these! *Give us an understanding heart* and everything else will follow!"

Now, in the sober reflection of our wide-awake hours, we repeat that we ask for nothing except the intelligence to understand that which is going on around us. No human being needs anything except an understanding heart, for with that comes all else that anyone can use.

Those who make it their business to meddle with economics will do well to remember that before there can be an equalized system of wealth distribution there must be an equalized system of intelligence distribution. Intelligence, an "understanding heart," is the power that controls every material thing on this earth, and one could no more change this law than he could stay the operation of the law of gravity and cause water to flow uphill unaided.

Get knowledge; get the ability to understand and interpret correctly all that goes on around you, and you will be able to get everything else you want. Intelligence rules this world. Get your share of it as quickly as you can.

Mr. Edison has become the world's leading inventor, not because he had more brains than other men who have not accomplished as much as he, but because he has developed an "understanding heart." Edison lives very close to Nature; he hears the sound of Nature's whisperings when and where men with better physical ears than his hear nothing at all. Mr. Edison has done nothing that any other normal man might not duplicate if he would develop the ability to interpret Nature's natural law as Edison has done. This ability is not a gift; it is an accomplishment, and the price that must be paid for it is persistent effort intelligently directed.

Oh to be a man with an understanding heart!

Down in Louisville, Kentucky, lives Mr. Cook, a man who has practically no legs and has to be wheeled around on a cart. Mr. Cook is the director of a great industry, a millionaire, all made by his own efforts. He has been a cripple since birth; that is, he has been crippled in his legs since birth.

In the City of New York one may see a strong, able-bodied and able-headed young man, without legs, rolling himself down Fifth Avenue every afternoon, with cap in hand, begging for a living.

This young man could duplicate anything that Mr. Cook, of Louisville, has done, *if he thought as Mr. Cook thinks*.

Henry Ford has more millions of dollars than he knows how to use. Not so many years ago he was working as a laborer in a machine shop, without education, with but little opportunity, without capital. Scores of other men, some of them with better organized brains than his, worked near him.

Ford threw off the poverty consciousness, *thought* of success and attained it. Every one of those other machinists could have done as well had they *thought* as Ford did.

Milo C. Jones, of Wisconsin, was stricken with paralysis. He could not even turn his body in bed without aid. He could not move. All of his limbs were practically useless, but there was nothing wrong with his brain, so it began to function in earnest, probably for the first time in its existence. Lying flat on his back in bed, Jones made that brain of his create a *definite* plan. That plan was prosaic and humble enough, but it was *definite* and it was a plan!

He decided to go into the sausage business. Calling his

family around him he told them of his plans and began directing them in carrying the plans into action.

With nothing to aid him except a sound mind Jones built an enormous sausage business and accumulated a big fortune in less than ten years of time. All this was accomplished after paralysis had stricken him down and made it impossible for him to earn a living with his hands or his physical body.

Where *thought* prevails power may be found!

The main difference between men is in the use to which they put their *thinking apparatus.* Intelligent thought carries men to the heights. Lack of it keeps them in misery, poverty and want all their lives.

Henry Ford makes millions of dollars because he first visioned millions of dollars and *demanded* of himself intelligent effort. The other machinists of Ford's early days visioned nothing but a weekly pay envelope and that was all they ever got. They demanded nothing of themselves that helped them get more than a weekly wage. If you want to get *more* be sure to *demand* more, but, make no mistake about it, *the demand must be made on yourself!*

Go out into the world where people are suffering, if you would learn about the emotions of the human heart. Find out what causes them to suffer; find out how much useless suffering they do, and why it is useless; find out how much their suffering is due to their own neglect or ignorance, and how much it is due to causes beyond their control. Find out what goes on in the heart of a little child when some brutal person beats it unmercifully, and, if you can do so find out what makes a grown-up beat a little child. Find out why some people try to close the gates of heaven to all who do not belong to their cult or creed, and, measure their action by your idea of Christianity and see if it squares up with the teachings of the Master. Read the Sermon on the Mount, in which will be found the Golden Rule, and find out why so few people have thought it worth their while to apply this precept. Find out what happens to a man, in his own heart, when, by intent or unfortunate circumstances, he offends society and is locked up in prison where nearly all of his personal liberty except that of eating and breathing is taken away from him. Find out if this improves him or makes him worse. Find out, also, why the majority of such men come out of prison with a firmly fixed intention of 'evening up' with someone for what they have suffered.

Find out what it is that causes people to want that which is forbidden.

II

SUCCESS

Success

The most popular word in the English language is *success!*

A few have achieved it; everybody wants to achieve it. Generally speaking, a man has succeeded when he has acquired all that he needs for his physical and spiritual well-being without having trespassed on the rights of his fellowmen.

However, no man ever succeeds in his own mind, because no man ever gets all that he wants. There is always something further ahead, just out of reach, that man wants but does not acquire. Perhaps this part of human nature is founded upon one of the laws through which evolution does its work. The two great urges that push man into action and keep him moving are the sex urge and the urge for the possession of material things or personal power.

Do not be alarmed if *you* are not satisfied. No man is ever fully satisfied, and if he were he would stop growing because he would stop struggling.

We contented ourselves, in the earlier days of this magazine, with the hope that someday we would have an audience of 100,000 readers, but soon we outgrew that limited hope and increased our vision so that we could see a million readers. The newly added lecture bureau will easily give us this bigger audience of a million, then we shall aim for two or perhaps three million.

The human mind is "fearfully and wonderfully made." Once you fix your mind on the achievement of a given end, and keep it fixed on that end with sufficient belief in your ability to attain it, unseen forces seem to ally themselves with you until you have *succeeded.*

Whatever success you attain will be attained through the proper use of your mind. Your physical, muscle power counts for *nothing.* Your mind power counts for *everything.*

The mastery of the air, with the aid of the flying machine, was a remarkable achievement, but it was an achievement of the brain and not the muscle. The thing was accomplished in the inventor's brain before it was demonstrated with the physical aid of the flying machine.

Harnessing the elements of the air and using them as a vehicle for conveying messages around the earth, without the aid of wires, was a wonderful achievement, but it was the work of the mind entirely.

You wish to succeed. It can do you no harm to know that *your* success must come through the aid of your own mind; especially the imaginative section of your mind wherein you build definite plans for the guidance of your physical activities.

Once in a great while success will seem to crown a man without effort on his part, through a stroke of favorable accidents, but most successful achievements come through organized effort, directed according to well organized plans.

The process of organizing your mind involves fifteen factors, as catalogued in the Magic Ladder to Success lecture. When you hear this lecture, or when you read it in printed form, be sure to analyze yourself, find out how many of these fifteen factors you need to add to those you are already using, organize your mind with the aid of these fifteen factors and your *success* will not be far away.

How Tactful Are You?

In the morning's mail we find a letter from a young writer who finds grievous fault with us because he came to our office seeking employment and failed to convince our assistant that she should turn him through the gate to the editorial sanctorum.

We have always admired persistence, but it is a dangerous thing unless directed with tact and diplomacy. Usually it is fatal to success if a salesman begins his effort to sell by provoking an argument with the man to whom he wishes to sell.

The letter that greets us from our aggrieved contemporary covers two pages of snappy and to some extent "clever" sentences, but the painful inescapable fact is that the letter convinces us of the soundness of our assistant's judgment in refusing the impromptu engagement. No writer who dips his pen in vitriol would make a suitable contributor to this magazine. Unconsciously this young writer has told us more about himself in his letter of protest than he could have told us in person had he been admitted, a fact which we mention for the purpose of showing how dangerous is the habit of giving away to anger.

Thought is the first faculty of man; to express it is one of his first desires; to spread it his dearest privilege.

Adaptability: the self-control to enable one to adapt oneself to any combination of circumstances, is a necessary qualification for achievement above mediocrity.

If you fail to get that which you go after you will be fortunate if you charge that failure to your own lack of ability to plan, or to your lack of powers of persuasion. You will be very unfortunate if, as our contemporary has done in the letter before us, you charge your failure to the man from whom you sought a favor or to whom you intended to make a sale.

The editor of this magazine is much more interested in purchasing suitable material for its pages than the writer of such material is in securing employment, but he cannot recall having ever purchased anything through coercion, or merely to please someone who had something to sell.

"Tact," said an old-fashioned Southern colored man, "is what most of us ain't got none of."

No man ever became a successful salesman without tact, and no man ever got very far in worldly achievement without good salesmanship. The friend who wrote us the letter expressing his annoyance at having called once without getting the opportunity to see the editor may be a clever writer, and his letter indicates that he is—in fact, a bit too "clever"—but he is not a clever *salesman,* and unless he learns to market his product he will need tons of paper and many garrets to hold his manuscripts, for his manuscripts will not sell themselves.

Ditto as to other classes of personal services!

We go through many long, lean and sometimes cruel years in gathering, classifying and coordinating facts and knowledge–in short, learning something. Then we must go through another period of years of salesmanship, trying to convince the world that we know something. Woe be unto the man who goes at this "convincing" task without the aid of tact and diplomacy.

Many a man has spoiled the chance of a lifetime by telling too much truth at one time, or at the wrong time, or by expressing his own opinion too arrogantly or too freely.

If we said that which we know to be the truth about the world in general and some of our acquaintances in particular, this would no longer be a Golden Rule Magazine, and we would be making enemies faster than we could fight them off.

While we know there is much that is wrong in the world we have elected to turn the spotlight on much that we know to be good, and this policy seems to have been a sound one for we are growing rapidly and serving well.

If you take notice of every event that does not please you your roadway in life will not be smooth. The more you show your resentment the more will people delight in giving you something to resent.

It's a good plan to develop tactfulness!

What Is a Leader Worth?

The Sales manager of a new organization was employed on a basis that enables him to earn $50,000.00 a year. One of the salesmen who works under the direction of this Sales manager objected because he, the salesman, could earn but half that amount.

There always has been and always will be a demand, at top-notch pay, for the man who can direct others, and such a man can practically set his own salary. No one can stop him. As a matter of fact it is difficult to stop a real leader of men in any reasonable task that he sets upon himself.

The young men of today show a new attitude toward women and marriage, an attitude of simplicity and frankness, a desire for mutual confidence, a readiness to discuss difficulties, an appeal to understand and be understood.
—Havelock Ellis

Carnegie made himself a multi-millionaire by selecting men who had leadership ability and then setting no limits on their pay. Schwab made himself one of the most powerful figures in the steel industry by the aid of this same principle. Perhaps Mr. Schwab could have purchased the services of Eugene Grace (now president of Bethlehem Steel Company) for fifty, or even twenty-five thousand dollars a year a few years back, but he preferred to give Mr. Grace all the responsibility he would assume and let him set his own income figures.

He is a wise leader of men who understands that it is a poor policy to beat men down to the lowest figure possible when purchasing their services. A much better plan is to select men who have undeveloped capacity along a given line and then place upon their shoulders sufficient responsibility and give them sufficient pay to bring out the best there is in them.

Fifty thousand dollars a year is none too much for the services of an efficient man who can intelligently and satisfactorily direct the efforts of a hundred men or so, helping each of them earn from five to ten times as much as he ever earned before or could earn under his own leadership.

How Can I Sell My Services?

The biggest market in the world is the market of personal services. Practically everyone has personal services for sale.

We are in receipt of a letter from a young lawyer who wants to know how he can build up a clientele without violating the ethics of his profession by direct advertising.

This is an excerpt from our reply, which may interest you:

"I started out to be a lawyer some fourteen years ago, therefore I know something of the predicament in which you find yourself.

"Now if I were in your place I would become an attractive public speaker and I would do my work so well that the newspapers would be compelled to give notice of it. I would find out what subjects were closest to the hearts of the people and I would prepare myself to talk authoritatively on those subjects.

"An able speaker always commands respect and attention. The newspapers cannot ignore him, even if they choose to do so, and the door of welcome is always open to him. This is one of the most effective ways for a professional man to place himself before the people, and if he avails himself of it with tact and skill he will soon find people making a beaten path to his door."

By all means learn to stand upon your feet and speak in public. If there is anything back of what you say you will soon find a demand for your services, no matter what may be your calling, greater than you can supply.

Like Attracts Like!

In the March issue of this magazine we devoted our most prominent page to eulogizing Dr. Robert K. Williams, who we thought deserved all we said about him.

Now Dr. Williams "retaliates" by not only eulogizing us, but he goes much further and actually renders us a service the value of which in dollars and cents we cannot yet estimate, but it is very great.

Had we used that prominent front page for the purpose of pointing out some weak spot in Dr. Williams' makeup he probably would have ignored us, but ninety-nine percent of humanity would have come back at us in a spirit of retaliation.

Dr. Williams came back at us, too, but he retaliated in kind. As a rule most men will do this. Slap a man in the face and if he does not slap you back right then and there he will do so, in one way or another, the first opportunity.

Speak a good word of a man and sooner or later he will retaliate in kind. If you understand how the human mind works you can get anyone to do practically anything that you have the right to ask him to do by first rendering that person some favor of an appropriate nature corresponding to the one you seek.

We know an advertising man who earns $25,000.00 a year. He admits that most of his ideas and all of his inspiration come from a man who earns but two thousand a year.

Not to understand and apply this law of the mind is to deprive yourself of one of the greatest forces with which you could ally yourself. You can actually utilize to advantage the energy in the minds of those with whom you come in contact providing you make the *right* move and make it *first!*

Many a man goes through life with a sort of unseen, but very much felt, *"kick me hard"* sign hanging on his back, for the reason that he is unconsciously and perhaps unintentionally irritating other people and causing them to strike back at him.

Fortunate is the man who has a few enemies, providing he has the intelligence to use their eyes and see himself as they see him. The eyesight of an enemy may be and usually is somewhat warped, but if you listen to what an enemy has to say about you there is no doubt that you will learn something that will help you improve yourself.

The law of retaliation is very real!

The magazine you hold in your hands is a splendid example of what can be accomplished through the use of the law of retaliation when it is directed to constructive, helpful ends. Through these pages we have said many nice things about many deserving people, and we have sent out nothing but positive, uplifting thoughts to inspire men and women to accomplish greater results from their efforts.

All these people who have read what we have written have retaliated, generally by interesting others in subscribing for the magazine, until the bulk of our daily receipt of subscriptions comes unsolicited, without cost.

It pays to say something good about folks; not alone in satisfaction, which is always in abundance, but in dollars as well. We thank you, Dr. Williams, for the service you have rendered us and *those who read what we had to say about you.*

The Servant Is Worthy of His Hire

Since the organization of our lecture bureau we have learned once more that the servant is worthy of his hire.

The majority of our lecture staff is being drawn from two sources: the clergy and the schools and colleges.

It is a well-known fact that neither the churches nor the schools pay their pastors and teachers enough to enable them to purchase all of the necessities of life, much less the luxuries.

We have clergymen on our lecture staff who have served the church for more than a quarter of a century. Many of them have sons and daughters to be educated, yet their pay has not been adequate to enable them to give their children the advantages of the best schools.

It is not surprising that a clergyman would want to direct his efforts into channels that would pay him enough to live on. The self-preservation instinct is a deeply seated one, and the man who serves the church is not different from the man who serves in other capacities in the that he wants to provide adequately for his family and at the same time lay by a competence for the time when he will no longer be able to serve at all.

Friendship is one of God's purest blessings to us...To divide one's heart into ten or twelve portions is very easy, very sweet, and very amiable.

—George Sand

Our lecture bureau has attracted some of the best men in the college field, and some of the most able clergymen, which is at one and the same time a compliment to our undertaking and a reprimand to those who ought to pay teachers and clergymen enough money to take care of their temporal needs.

If *your* pastor should announce from his pulpit next Sunday morning that he has decided to leave the service of your church and ally himself with our lecture bureau you should reprimand yourself and your fellow churchmen and not your pastor, for he is perhaps moved by the desire to serve on a wider scale and at the same time provide more liberally for his family.

If you want to hold your clergymen and your teachers the first step is to pay them what they are worth, or at least somewhere near as much as they could earn in other fields of endeavor. If you fail to do this you are sure to lose their services sooner or later.

This same principle perhaps applies quite as appropriately in the field of business and industry. If a business firm has an exceptionally efficient servant, whether he is an executive capacity or working as a day laborer, it should be someone's business to see that this servant is paid in proportion to his ability to produce results.

Men of the idealistic type, such as most clergymen are, will serve with never a thought of compensation for a time, but economic pressure and growing families and increasing cost of living all combine to force them finally to resort to more profitable fields.

The servant is worthy of his hire. Give it to him before your competitor does.

III

LEADERSHIP

Leadership

This is the shortest editorial we ever wrote, but it carries one of the biggest ideas we ever had: Before you can GET that which you call success, you must GIVE something of equal value in return. Set it down as a sure thing that which you hand the world, whether it is efficient service or poor service, grouchiness or good cheer. If you get this viewpoint and make proper use of it you will enjoy success this coming year such as you never experienced before.

Leadership

In one of the great cities a large factory building caught fire. Hundreds of girls, working on the upper floors, were in danger of death. The whole lower floor was in flames and the blazes were rolling up the fire escapes, cutting off all avenue of escape.

The crowd stood on the outside waiting for the firemen to arrive!

In that crowd was a young man who was different from all the others. He took in the situation, hurriedly measured the distance with his eyes from the burning building to another building just across the alley, then, just as if he were in full charge he began to give orders to the bystanders and in a few minutes he had rustled a crew of six strong men.

He led the way and they followed him to the top of the adjoining building. On his way up he had picked up a rope and his six followers had torn down a bill board and carried the planks to the top of the other building.

This self-appointed leader threw one end of the rope to a women in the window of the burning building and instructed her to fasten it. He scaled the rope, carrying one end of a plank with him. His six helpers pushed out the boards they had carried up and soon they had completed a very substantial bridge from one building to the other.

When the firemen arrived nearly one-third of the occupants

of the burning building were out of danger!

No one invited this young man to become a leader!

Leadership is something which seldom comes by invitation. It is something which you must invite yourself into. In every business there is a fine opening for a first-class leader. But, he must be a man who is willing to do the thing that ought to be done without someone telling him to do it.

One of the men who stood in that little crowd of people and watched the flames as they threatened the women in the building, in speaking of the incident afterward, said "Aw, that was nuthin'; anybody could a done that if he'd a tried!"

And he was right! Anybody could have had that glorious job as leader, merely by stepping up and taking it, but the fact remains that *only one* man out of the whole crowd saw the opportunity and was willing *to take the risk* that went with it.

Leadership means responsibilities, it is true, but the most profitable work usually is that which shoulders the greatest responsibility on a man.

Wherever there is work to be done you can find a chance to become a leader. It may be humble leadership, at first, but leadership becomes a habit and soon the most humble leader becomes a powerful man of action and he is then sought for greater leadership.

Look back down the ages and history will tell you that leadership was the quality which thrust greatness upon the men of the past.

Washington, Lincoln, Patrick Henry, Foch, Roosevelt, Dewey, Haig, and Woodrow Wilson—leaders, all!

We must BE before we can DO, and we can do only to the extent that we ARE, and what we ARE depends upon what we THINK.

None of these were invited to become leaders. They stepped into leadership by their own aggressiveness. None of them started at the top. Most of them began in the most lowly capacity, but, they formed the habit of doing that which needed to be done, *whether it was their job to do it or not; whether they were paid for it or not!*

If you are one of the great majority who have made up their minds not to do anything which is not their job, and for which they are not paid, there is no hope of leadership crowning your efforts.

Frank A. Vanderlip was a stenographer not so many years ago. We do not know for sure, but we suspect that he did not confine his efforts to the work which his stenographic position required, for if he had he would never have been the leader of finance which he is today.

James J. Hill was a telegraph operator, but had he insisted on working union hours only and had he delivered no more service than was required to hold the job of telegrapher, he never would have been the great railroad builder that he was.

Leadership! What a wonderful privilege it is to be a leader! What a wonderful opportunity there is in every shop, factory, crossroads grocery store and business establishment to become a leader by merely doing the thing that ought to be done whether you are told to do it or not.

IV

THE POWER OF EXTENDED VISION

The Power of Extended Vision

Once this writer went to the mountains to gather chestnuts. We took a gallon bucket with us to bring back the chestnuts in.

Before starting we had "visualized" a gallon bucket of chestnuts; we had prepared to bring back just one gallon and no more.

When we got to the mountains we found bushels of chestnuts on the ground, but we had to come away and leave them there because we had not thought in larger numbers when we planned the trip.

We have thought of that chestnut-hunting trip many a time in the years which followed.

We could have brought back a bushel sack full of chestnuts just as easily as we brought the gallon bucket full if we had extended our *"vision"* before we started on the trip.

Every time we see a person beginning a new enterprise we think of that chestnut-hunting trip, because we know that most people are making the same mistake that we made, in not thinking in large enough terms.

In planning our Chief Aim in the years gone by we can plainly see, now, that we never achieve more than we aimed to achieve. We doubt if it would have been possible to accomplish more than we started out to accomplish.

Happy, contented workmen usually are a mere reflection of the disposition of the head of the works.

Now and then an unusually ambitious person will take along more vessels, when he starts "chestnutting," than will be needed, but generally the reverse is true. It is the same in planning a professional career, or building a business, or developing an education.

You may accomplish less than that which you visualized in

your plans, but you will *never* accomplish more! You will never sell more goods than you planned to sell; you will never become more famous in any profession than you plan to become; you will never stand higher in the estimation of your fellow men than you aim to stand; therefore, it seems worthwhile to extend one's vision every now and then, so it will cover more territory.

It is not probable, in beginning any business or profession, that you will see all the possibilities ahead of you when you lay out your first set of plans, but as time goes on you will be able to extend your vision and make your aims cover more territory.

This power of extended vision is something which you must cultivate.

The power of extended vision is the only power on earth, which will help a person to climb out of the rut of mediocrity in any walk of life.

May the gods of fate help the person who lacks this power of extended vision, because he has not cultivated it or encouraged its growth and development.

The man or woman who does not periodically extend his or her vision so that it covers more territory, takes in larger numbers, causes him or her to think in bigger terms, may be likened to a horse that has been broken and harnessed to do service as a heavy draft horse. One reason why such a horse never tries to break away from his unfortunate lot, is his lack of extended vision. He accepts his fate with complacency, never once imagining that no man on earth could master him if he could think and plan how to throw off the harness.

There are a number of people in this world–many millions all told, we suspect–who are harnessed and hitched to mediocre, depressing, soul-crushing work which merely provides an existence, for no other reason than the lack of *extended vision!*

If this is true, or even approximately so, what an ugly indictment it is against our system of educating men and women. If the simple process of extending one's vision so as to cause one to aim at greater accomplishments is really of value, what a distressing pity it is that this fact is not brought out more clearly in every educational institution in the world.

This writer may be laying too much stress upon this subject; he may be giving it too important a place among the list of qualities which one must possess in order to enjoy success in this world, but he has a mighty sound reason for his views on the subject.

For twenty-two years, ever since we were thrown upon our own responsibility in the world, we have been watching with unusual interest, those experiences which have done most to help us acquire the necessities of life, and we are forced to the conclusion that the ability to extend one's vision and expect more of one's self is not only a *desirable* quality, but a *necessary* one!

You may never have heard of the incident which was directly responsible for our being able to get out of the dirty, unprofitable work of laborer in a coal mine, but if you have you will be patient if we repeat it for the benefit of those who have not heard it.

That incident took place some twenty-two years ago!

No incident in our whole life has been of more lasting benefit to us than this one, because it gave us the starting point of this idea concerning the power of *extended vision!*

We were sitting before the fire one night, after the hard day's work was over, talking of our splendid new job which paid us a dollar a day!

We were proud of that job!

A dollar a day for a boy of our age was a lot of money; more, in fact, than we had ever seen before, that we could call our own.

In our boyish enthusiasm and exuberance we said something which impressed the old gentlemen with whom we were talking. He reached over, took us firmly by the shoulder, gripped it so hard that we almost yelled with pain, looked us squarely in the eyes and said: "Why, you are a bright boy! If you'd go to school and get yourself an education you'd *make your mark in the world!"*

That was the first time in our life that any one had ever told us that we were "bright," or, that we could "make our mark in the world." Up to that time we had never thought in larger terms than $2.50 a day. We were receiving $1.00 a day for our labor, but aspired to receive the same as some of the older men were, our limit of "extended vision" at that time being $2.50 a day in wages, with never a thought of being anything except a coal mine laborer.

That remark by that good old gentleman gave us a jolt!

We paid no attention to it at first, but we began to think it over that night after we had retired, we retraced our experiences in our mind. We remembered the bright luster in the old man's eyes as he made this remark. There was something about his whole action and demeanor which aroused us to understand that he was not speaking of impossibilities.

To control thought is the secret of all progress on this earth, and that power is YOURS if you will exercise it.

That remark caused us to extend our vision so that we could see beyond the coal mine in which we worked. It caused us to begin to look beyond the village limits in which we coal miners were located, into another village where there was a school. But, most important of all, it sowed seed in our mind which took root and began to grow; seed which we have harvested and transplanted into other minds in many thousands of cases since that memorable night, twenty-two years ago.

This editorial, and the magazine you hold in your hands, may be traced directly back to that two-minute conversation during which I got my first impression of the power of extended vision.

If your lot in life is unsatisfactory, as it no doubt is, you will be well paid for the time you have devoted to reading this editorial, if you will right about face and draw another and much larger circle which will represent your *extended vision!* Let that circle take in more territory than any you have yet drawn. Let it cover the position or station in life which you seek. Remember that your possibilities of achievement are strictly confined to the limits of that boundary line which may be called your line of vision.

When a modern industrial plant outgrows its housing quarters, the management, if it is sound and progressive, immediately looks for more space and enlarge the plant.

You must do the same with reference to your personal efforts, if you are to overcome that undesirable station in life in which you find yourself.

To feel dissatisfied with your lot in life is a normal, healthy indication; but, to remain where you are, with no attempt to enlarge your vision or plan ways and means of transplanting yourself into a larger field is abnormal and indicates an unhealthy condition of mind.

One of the chief aims of this magazine is to cause its readers to think in bigger, broader and more progressive terms! There is nothing which we can do that will be of benefit to you except that which we can help you do for *yourself!*

Get away into some quiet spot!

Sit down for a few minutes and take inventory of yourself. Find out whether or not you are acquiring more knowledge, developing more self-confidence, widening your circle of vision, setting heavier tasks for yourself; expecting more of yourself than you were a year ago. If you are not there is room for alarm.

One of the reasons why failure is a blessing is that it often cause us to stop, look and *reason!* It often causes us to find out some weakness or shortcoming which we had never suspected ourselves of possessing.

This writer is particularly thankful for the mistakes he has made in the past twenty-two years, and for his failures in many undertakings which had they been successful, would have directed his efforts toward work which would have been less profitable to posterity than the work he is now doing.

Many of our mistakes worked a temporary hardship on others, and all of them worked an *immediate* hardship on us, but these mistakes and failures were profitable, because every one of them caused us to climb up out of the debris of the failure itself with a broader and more extended vision than we had before.

Fires are usually destructive, but it is a well known fact that it takes a first-class fire to give many a town its first real growth. The fire comes along and burns out the old, timeworn buildings. This works a hardship on many; some have no insurance and others less insurance than they should have had, but, as a whole, the fire is a blessing, because the owners replace the old buildings with newer and more artistic ones, which add to the appearance of the town and the value of the property.

Many a man needs the reactionary effect of some sort of a "fire" of failure that will sweep away the old, time-worn, inadequate plans which have been holding him down, and give him a chance to extend his vision and build a newer, more progressive and artistic plan that will be wider in scope.

One afternoon this writer was sitting in his office, in Dallas, Texas, some time ago. He looked down the hall and saw a very pleasant looking young man coming toward him, with a salesman's portfolio in his hands. He was stopped at the information desk, but the writer told the boy at the desk to send him on in.

When he was seated inside of my office, I said to him: "I do not know what you are selling, and whatever it is I probably will not be a purchaser, but there is one thing about you that is valuable; you have a pleasing personality."

The young man thanked me, then informed me that he was selling electric foot-warmers for the Dallas Electric Light Company. I told him that I needed no foot-warmers, as I was seldom troubled with "cold feet," but, I suggested that he ought to be selling something that would give him a larger profit on each sale. I suggested to him that with a personality such as he had, with the self-confidence that he possessed, he ought to be able to sell anything that he tried.

This young man was not in my office more than five minutes, but during those five minutes something happened that will make a mighty big difference to him all of his life. He thanked me for my compliment and went away.

About three weeks later the manager of the electrical service department of the Dallas Electric Light Company came to see me. He informed me that I had been the cause of his losing one of his best men, and when I asked how that happened, he said that the young man whom I have mentioned, whose name was Brown, came right back to the office that very day, turned in his sales kit, went out and got a job which paid him much more money, and he was making good in that new job in a big way.

I said to my visitor that I regretted that I was the cause of his losing a good man, but I was proud that Mr. Brown had learned the value of "extended vision."

Mr. Stuart Austin Wier, of Dallas, was sitting in my office at the time and heard the conversation. After my visitor had gone, Mr. Wier turned to me and asked:

"What sort of a shot did you inject into Brown's arm?"

And I replied: "The same sort of a shot that I wish I might have the opportunity of shooting into the arm of every person in the world whose lot in life is unfortunate, and who is chained to work which is both unpleasant and unprofitable."